*For Jane —
So honored to
present @ your first
reading — launched!*

AMERICAN RUSH
SELECTED POEMS

*love,
Maureen
2000
NYC
bluestocking
Bookstore*

by Maureen Owen

Country Rush (1973)
The No-Travels Journal (1975)
a brass choir approaches the burial ground (1977)
Hearts in Space (1980)
AE (Amelia Earheart) (1984)
Zombie Notes (1985)
Imaginary Income (1992)
Untapped Maps (1993)
American Rush: Selected Poems (1998)

Maureen Owen

American Rush

Selected Poems

Talisman House, Publishers
Jersey City, New Jersey

Copyright © 1998 by Maureen Owen
All rights reserved

Published in the United States of America by
Talisman House, Publishers
P.O. Box 3157
Jersey City, New Jersey 07303-3157

Manufactured in the United Sates of America
Printed on acid-free paper

Acknowledgements: The works in this collection are taken from *Country Rush* (Adventures in Poetry Press, 1973), *No-Travels Journal* (Cherry Valley Editions, 1975), *a brass choir approaches the burial ground* (Big Deal 5, 1977), *Hearts in Space* (Kulchur Foundation, 1980), *Zombie Notes* (Sun Press, 1985), *Imaginary Income* (Hanging Loose Press, 1992), and *Untapped Maps* (Potes & Poets Press, 1993). The original edition of *Country Rush* had a cover and drawings by Yvonne Jacquette. The *No-Travels Journal* was originally published in an edition of 500 copies with cover and drawings by Hugh Kepets. Some of the poems in *Imaginary Income* were first published in a pamphlet by Potes and Poets Press. Many of these poems first appeared in alternative, independent small press poetry magazmes. The Kohoutek poem on page 51 originally appeared as a broadside illustrated by Britton Wilkie. The brush and ink drawing on the title page of the Country Rush section is by Joe Giordano.

The cover illustration is a detail from "My American Family,"
#6 in a series of photo collages, "Luke's Home," by Laura Goolden.
Used by permission of the artist.

Library of Congress Cataloging-in-Publication Data

Owen, Maureen, 1943-
    American rush : selected poems / Maureen Owen.
        p. cm.
    ISBN 1-883689-70-8 (acid-free paper). -- ISBN 1-883689-69-4 (pbk. : acid-free paper)
    I. Title
PS3565.W558A83   1998
811'.54--dc21   98-16329
                                                                                   CIP

for Peter Ganick, Bob Hershon, Bill Zavatsky,
Bonnie Lateiner, Lita Hornick, Barbara Baracks,
Pam and Charlie Plymell, and Larry Fagin . . .

those courageous and tireless
independent publishers of poetry
who have published the books
of the works herein over the years
and made this collection possible.

Contents

FROM *Country Rush* (1973) ❦ 1

Country Place ❦ 3
Digging Sassafras in July ❦ 4
"The thing to do when you meet ❦ 5
That Summer ❦ 6
Delirious Orchard ❦ 7
There's No Gold in the Kitchen ❦ 8
Shyness is a strange disease ❦ 9
Goodyear ❦ 10
Farming Country ❦ 12
The fertilizer plant burst ❦ 13
Silent Film ❦ 14
Gravel Rash ❦ 15
Hot Bath! ❦ 16
Body Rush ❦ 17
Dear L, ❦ 18
Survival Song ❦ 19
Land O Lakes ❦ 20

FROM *The No-Travels Journal* (1975) ❦ 21

FROM *a brass choir approaches the burial ground* (1977) ❦ 49

I walk into doors ❦ 51
Love Song for T. ❦ 53
Who Needs It ❦ 54
How To Get By ❦ 56
Go ahead   Spit the mushrooms ❦ 57
Fantasy 22 ❦ 59
Up in the Air ❦ 60
"Wanting You" ❦ 61
When you're down and under ❦ 62

Traveling ❖ 63
Thank you, America ❖ 64
Be careful not to say too quickly ❖ 65
Just because the sea is calm ❖ 66
"She's a real tough cookie" ❖ 68
O Alkaline sap of the Ash ❖ 69
Yellow Yo-Yo's ❖ 70

FROM *Hearts in Space* (1980) ❖ 71

Handscroll with ink and colours on silk ❖ 73
"Dearest Bupple" ❖ 74
"Some days," ❖ 76
Monica ❖ 78
Ode to Asexuality ❖ 79
The baby bangs his forehead ❖ 80
All That Glitters ❖ 81
"To be without humor" ❖ 83
Goodbye September ❖ 85
For Beethoven who played ❖ 86
Poem to Piss Everyone Off ❖ 87
for Emily (Dickinson) ❖ 88
"I truly believe that we are enchanted" ❖ 89
The little dwarf boy ❖ 91
Frogs Ringing Gongs in a Skull ❖ 92

FROM *Zombie Notes* (1985) ❖ 93

Saran Wrap ❖ 95
"stone letter in a pot" ❖ 96
Days & Nights ❖ 97
When he said "petit air" ... ❖ 98
"Can I Still Love You   & Hate The Word Husband" ❖ 100
Novembers   or straight life ❖ 102
We Can't Find the Traitor But Of Course ❖ 103
in my dream   my grandmother ❖ 104
Tutankhamun's coffin weighed 2,448 pounds ❖ 105
A Piece ❖ 106
Because   Therefore   So ❖ 107

Winter is so   punk • 108
Poems Without Names   or your plane takes off • 109
for Ulysses on his high school graduation • 110
Letters to the Letters S and F • 111

FROM *Imaginary Income* (1992) • 117

sexuality because of sexism is a problem for most women • 119
Soffits & Fascias • 120
Blue Nile • 121
O • 122
tall white & densely fluid • 123
Martha • 124
seeing him's like standing on a hot plate • 125
how I feel is cool   very cool • 126
So muchos the story & tale it goes • 127
Always the word "love" written in vanishing ink . . . vanishing • 128
Dashboard Idol • 129
We • 130
the happiest parts were the parts she made up • 131
Talking to distract the listener . . . • 132
rain dents a steady robust • 133

FROM *Untapped Maps* (1993) • 135

to fly • 137
In August 1874 Manet stayed • 138
What do you do when you can't • 139
Something just out of reach • 140
Maybe the stars were crossed • 141
From Gossip Notes of Court Life • 142
Trash Stars • 143
Anchorage to Nome • 144
FOR KYRAN • 145
I had eaten too much sugar • 146
STANDING BEAUTY WITH SLEEVE IN • 147
Topography • 150

American Rush
Selected Poems

FROM *Country Rush* (1973)

COUNTRY PLACE

That's it!

to the blue smoky evening
a memento!

Don't get up.

I know the exact method
so
Now I'm standing in front
of cylindrical wood stacks

Instant green bugs
have landed on the reddish
cedar bark

dogs in the valley begin to bark
& one by one the lights come on

When I lift the log
those bugs will take off
their bright green dissolving
in woodlands and hundreds of hills.

DIGGING SASSAFRAS IN JULY

In Buddhist hierarchy all living things are bound
to go   so I'm sorry little sassafras tree
I need your roots for tea & I'm sorry medium-sized
black ants   I need your house for tea   I'm sorry
Turkish-amber forest for this mess!   splintered
bark   horrible hole in earth   fallen body
of young tree   stripped   I need these leaves for
Gumbo   this is no survival test   even the sky
loses out in the end to space   I know I'm just
another ambition stepping all over the moss   &
You'd have done better to be born a diamond!   a
potentiality we all assume to be greater than our own!
for instance   Diamonds are a girl's best friend!
DIAMONDS!   If I can't walk on citrine   malachite   or
turquoise   then I'll just sit down here under the
Paulownia trees
            & O Ambergris!

leaves in bucket   roots in brown sack
sweating in early morning haze   The sun will dry
the digging   woodbine and termite will clear the
remains   & when we leave   this wondrous   odor of
root beer   will hang in the branches for days . . .

*"The thing to do when you meet
the Buddha is to eat him."*

The first thing I did when I arrived in
the country was to rush out into a grassy
meadow & start eating.
Grass, golden dandelions, thistles, little
bluish clover flowers & stalks, enormous
weeds.   I feasted
I ate my way into the grove devouring trees
saplings, stumps, bird nests, caterpillars,
I was rapacious!   & giddy
I gulped, masticated, stored acorns in my
cheeks, ate fallen twigs, old pieces of
harness, abandoned dog bones, I ate the tiger
lilies, the snowball bush my grandmother had
planted, I ate the garden gate, old fence posts,
storm warnings, tractors, plows, combines,
wheat fields, oats, corn cribs, I ate my way
to the house then I ate the house, the barn,
the chicken coop & the chickens, the granary,
the cows, with gusto I scarfed the clouds, the
gesturing plumhued sky, the neighbors,
I ate the farmer & his faithful dog Alice,
I burped   & returned to the city.

THAT SUMMER

for Gary Snyder

there were beetles,
junebugs, praying mantis,
sweat bees, fireflies, tit mice,
scarabs, seed ticks, ants,
brown recluse spiders,
katydids, damselflies, grubs,
copperheads, scorpions, tumble bugs,
ground bees, garter snakes, pigmy
rattlers, chickadees, ladybugs,
house centipedes, sulfur butterflies,
daddy-long-legs, fruit flies,
gnats, frogs, caterpillars, waterbugs,
tarantulas, flickers, cicadas,
mud daubers, luna moths, black racers,
turtles, bitterns, bot flies, wheel bugs,
quail, trap door spiders, dragonflies,
cardinals, walking sticks, toads, hornets,
purple grackles, great blue herons,
possums, nut hatches, robins, moles,
flying squirrels, monarch butterflies,
swallows, turkey vultures, may flies,
speckled king snakes, orb spiders,
hog-nosed snakes, barn owls,
rain crows, woodthrush, raccoon,
grasshopper, rabbit, Cooper's hawk,
Saw-Whet owls, horse flies, pileated
woodpeckers, mosquitoes, mice, wild duck,
fish, bald eagles, red fox, woodchucks,
skunk, bumble bee, black vulture,
turtle dove, cricket, & screech owl.

DELIRIOUS ORCHARD

An active aura   gets me out of bed
bathed in sunlight   benefits of the third dimension
downstairs on TV   There goes the Lunar Rover!
heading toward the rim of Hadley Rille
beautiful geology—radio samples & the wide angle pan
whatever that means   "By gosh" & "Yeah man"
I'm excited   LOOK AT THAT ROCK!
"a double core!"   ready to roll
parked below St. George Crater
there's no sweet clover on the moon   no wild alfalfa
not even a sow thistle   but we observe the little
patterns of the past   against the chaos of infinity

Will the moon reciprocate our affection?
Will robust platinum cheeks give us a smile?
OH MOON!
         Here on earth   I lean back a lot
take a drag of pure fresh air & stare up into
your friendly skies.

THERE'S NO GOLD IN THE KITCHEN

       Another evening   ruined   Complaints about
the food   the bath   the delicately scented
massage oils   Even the Rapture   amiss!
& getting into bed I stepped on your ankle again
The mind proceeds through addition   not synthesis
adding and adding and adding and adding and adding
everything up!   The enormous porch   the
terrible stairway   the awesome facade of internal
trials   the gruesome heavy lock to be opened
& after that   the endless hall
        When will we ever reach Antarctica
and stroll in amazement over the underground waterfalls!
where   ice-blue in the mantle of swirling sheets
we convert these public characters into private myth
leaping through the door!   towards the
monumental dignity of two   fleeing across the highway
leaving morals   ideals   and ethics behind   & taking
with them   violence   quick device   & luck
to a locality instead
to the edge of a temporary thing
                          O tortured Souls!
at odds between the kitchen & weird adventure
Don't worry
          We read your memoirs   O we are tortured too!
& draw these parallels between us.

Shyness is a strange disease I have
it may require surgery some day
Propped up in a big white hospital bed
it will be strange to feel the big toe
on my left foot gone
But how wonderful to be no longer shy
only slightly off balance
Perhaps I'll develop the limping stride
of Byron
people stepping back as I jerk through

GOODYEAR

       A view so carefully attained   it roared
       avalanche lilies sprang up between our toes
       "Let's sleep in the garden." you said.
       "Let's sleep in the lighthouse," you said
       "Let's sleep in the fruitcellar, the orchard,
       the cannon, the stable, the armchair, the oven,
       the backseat, the Southwest,   the beaver pond—"
       love like an assortment of chapters   a spiritual epidemic
       it was biting & furious   a vituperative sea
       that washed in to blunder the details of life.

       The cadence of morning evaporates dreams' limitations
       a certain quality about you has been noticeable for years.
       That dream I had about you   that dream!
       it was musical   it came out of the air I breathed
       I was experiencing the relief of experience
       inlaid
       with quadrangular illustrations of emotion
       I was free!
                     going or coming or coming back
       to you
       who will glance up one day
       from your diurnal tasks to see
       what I was like before I changed.

       I am giving away the vendetta
       to a passing Shaman   opals madly flogging his forehead.
       It was Joshu who took off his shoe   put it on his head

       & walked out of the room.

So the process of seduction follows every new idea

                Being a great dresser
                                  a great dancer
   a sea swallow
                    a vase in winter

Incidents while we stood under the drupaceous branches
fondling mammoth peaches with our tongues.

FARMING COUNTRY

        The true measure of reality   an attitude
        at right angles with each chubby grove &
        solitary cottonwood   little clumps clamped
        on the horizon   a state of mind   because
        I'm so glad it's a spoon & not a saucer   that
        whirrs through salubrious kitchen air
        such a typical variation of your love
        folks here swig beer   swap tales   continuously
        assessing the likelihood that several events
        are related   a repeated & regular significance
        surrounded by the whooping of the wind   find
        happiness in the things that should really make
        you happy & out on these plains   it's VELOCITY
        a craze for speed!
                        Full throttle!   dead run
        hot pursuit   make tracks   eat my dust
        stretch your legs!   bite the wind   take off
        speed up!   really traveling!
                        HERE IS A THEME
        which is like saying   there's a lot of room
        & the land's so flat here   I'm perpendicular

The fertilizer plant burst into flame
devouring an entire network of expectations.
In the Spring the carpenters lifted big hammers
& thought of Ma & Pa Kettle
discovering uranium in their well.
Monochrome visions of sparkling teeth
gather in the evening clouds.
Ma & Pa sit on their front porch, as we do
watching the smoke jump convulsively from
the burning fertilizer plant.
A tragic figure looming over the Great Plains
the Sacred Buffalo relinquishes his shape
to desultory breezes.
Now & then a variation blows the smoke into
our eyes.

SILENT FILM

I love you when I go to the movies.
When the pallid fiancée clasps the
inlaid box containing the lover's
severed hand   to her breast
the foamflower estuary stutters in the choppy wind
a low tide affected with hiccuping whitecaps
tributaries of compassion jolt into my fingertips
love's panic   I want to jump up & dash home
to you!   But the movies are so magnetic—
& they cost plenty too   I keep my seat.
Her new lover is a snob!
      "My hands have to be in the mood, actually,"
      zipping up
      "I'm no cold potato, it's just temperament,
      that's all."
Also his balance is poor   & enraged
at the contents of the box
he turns himself into an auto one afternoon
& runs the poor girl down
The lovely box   is flung   unhinged
among shattered mother-of-pearl
on a stony beach   the hand
disguised as a horseshoe crab   climbs out
& scuttles   into   the   sea.

GRAVEL RASH

        From my window   in the north bedroom
        pinkish light rectangles into gladiolus
        cars pop by on the road from Rainbow Island
        under these stars   full of beer & power
        big men that work on that road coming back

                  OH Night Driver
                     Come on!
          every car that goes by on the road is you!

HOT BATH!

        the frog-shaped girl with swollen eyes
        is taking a bath with the noise of seven camels
        beads of oil & perspiration hang in the little
        hairs of her nose
        She is red as a pair of dilapidated flannels.

        her sheer draped skin dissolves
        then the veins & pulpy muscles float out
        until finally
        her unsupported bones fall forward
        into the water   & melt!

BODY RUSH

I'm taking a ride with you   in my head
true Love & Oh!   the cornfield!

a sweet girl

                                      (Maybe an understanding of the life
will help)

          This wind blows over your body
          comes across the fields & blows over
          my body!   Doesn't that bother you?

              TOO MUCH

I'm thinking of you   it's you in my head   you're on my mind
I can't get you out of my etc.   Can't shake you loose
can't stop thinking of you   I haven't washed you out of
my hair   I expect you every night   Don't you *like*
blow jobs?   Time is short   but I wait for you
I'm crazy about you   I'm in love with you
    You blow my mind
        Come by!
                Drop in!
Let's rap!
        Let's neck   Pussy is delicious!
   What are you waiting for?
You're beautiful
                lusty   handsome
   Your vibes are tremendous!
                         I can't believe it!

for Lauren

Dear L,
    Thanks for the early guided hike down to the bottom lands through juniper & hawthorn, grapevine, sassafras, hackberry, honeysuckle, red oak, slippery elm, paw paw, trumpet vine, crape myrtle, boxelder, virginia creeper, wild plum, smoke bush, golden raintree, black gum, post oak, sugar maple, linden, fern, mulberry, winged elm, ashe juniper, red birch, hickory, witch hazel, woolly buckthorn, ash, American elm, walnut, wild ginger, red bud, silver maple, viburiaum, sumac, spice bush, lichen, dogwood, chinquapin, honey locust, false solomon seal, wild cherry, orange root, black haw, cedar, white oak, pine, wild current, bass wood, moss, elephant ear, legume, green briar, blasted oak, poison ivy, mumbling bee, red maple, scary mustard seed & wild catalpa on the last day of our visit.

SURVIVAL SONG

      Don't worry about me   on latenight subways
coming home down snowy abandoned blvds.
I am La Coyote   she of the white track
loping through thick drifts   the stinging
crystals at my eyes   muggers drop their arms
at my approach   murderers withdraw back into
doorways   shivering   as my shadow floats over
the snow   trotting soundlessly up second ave
"German Shepherd," someone says to calm his
startled companion   but really I am La Loba
the she-wolf   a low hum in my throat
a terrible power in my yellow eyes   junkies
quiver   haggard & dangerous con men
skirt widely as I pass them moving at a low run
down 110th   perverts howl & race for cover
I am La Coyote   invisible in the deepening snow
no one touches me   I make it home   everytime.

LAND O LAKES
for Minnesota

    The Grassland Wolf Spider is still behind the large
blue framed mirror in the bathroom
You are a nomad I told him this morning   Go out
into the grasslands!   Fear has ruined everything here.
I lost my knife and the dog is worthless
like a brilliant and sensational misunderstanding
THE GREAT EMPTINESS   is out there   decorated with
celestial grandeur   the capacity for dominating whole moments
in those stars   European architecture
and the Abode of the Unsymmetrical
     Oh romantic eaves & open spaces!   I rush
through hordes of mosquitoes and kiss the toes of your
reckless empty beauty!   my life on dirt roads
flushed & dizzy   bathed in a cold sweat   Nature's
out & out extravagance   What a beautiful evening!
someone will say   & I'll just collapse.

FROM *The No-Travels Journal* (1975)

"It seems to me that I should always be happier elsewhere than where I happen to be, and this question of moving is one that I am continually talking over with my soul."

Charles Baudelaire
Petits Poemes en Prose
translated by Arthur Symons

LILY OF THE FIELD

On Monday I wore the red green purple & gold sectioned sweater Tandy gave me   the pantaloons I made from the green velvet R gave me   the green yellow orange & royal blue scarf Tessie crocheted for us last christmas   the red leather boots Lauren bought me   the red green blue black & yellow mirror cloth bag Jan sent me from California   with plush red band I made from the velvet I ripped off on first ave & the grey felt Charles Dickens coat I got on Ave B for $1.50

On Tuesday I wore the cotton square dancing dress Sandy sent from Iowa   the red white & blue american flag earrings I gave me last summer and that I repainted at Rebecca's with Turan's model airplane enamel   the perfectly good gloves I found in the trash   same boots the beautiful warm red socks I ripped off from Woolworth's and the curly brown Atlantic fur coat I found in a trunk in my uncle's attic summer before last

On Wednesday I wore the skinny knit button-up my mother gave me   & that I tie-died myself with Darlene's Rit Dye   The long fringed gypsy skirt of loose orange crochet you can completely see through that Judi bought for me in Italy   the vermilion green violet ocher and white stripped scarf with gold and white stripes between the other stripes & black tassels on turquoise strings that Rebecca brought me from Turkey   the same boots   the clove and peppercorn beads J made me   the cape Brett gave me in Kyoto   & my terrific little antique copper-mail purse that we traded the books for in the mountains

On Thursday I wore the amber sweater Katie handed down to me over the black velvet top I got at Royal Rags for 25 cents the violet suede belt Arlette ripped off for me   the baggy white sailor pants I found in my grandmother's dresser that had been my uncle's when he was in the navy 20 years before the same grey felt coat and a pair of perfect-fit tennis shoes someone had left here

On Friday I wore the yellow dress Adam gave me when he was working at the cleaners & no one came to pick it up   the cinnabar cork shoes Lauren bought for me   the velvet cape I made and trimmed with the gold stuff T gave me when she moved the Shaman's cap that George's mother picked up in Brazil and that katie gave us last christmas & the little purse D brought me that was made in Israel from the material left over after they make the dresses and that has red green yellow & orange tassels and bright wolf-pink embroidery on the inside

Today is Saturday   I get up & put on the earrings I made
from the ivory plating off the piano keys you gave me
on the coast   the orange & grey diagonally striped neck
scarf K gave me   the powerful sun & moon medallion from
Peru   & the opaque sky-blue beads I stung into a headband
I look at myself in the mirror   a long time   then get dressed.
I wear the torn black velvet gown   covering the tears with
the tiny silver bells from India that L bought for me in
Oklahoma   & the yellow tights.   I wear M's battered and
softened old brown boots   Do I really embody all the faults
you keep telling me I have?   I go to the park with the children
we run through the weak grass   the bare brown mounds.
Is it expanded household life that causes me to long for
Europe.   for the Caspian Sea?
                O continent of Asia, I am sitting here
in the park on these sparkling boulders & only the economy
of the nation   is keeping us apart!

Coming by foot across 109th   girls in tight colors &
embroidered jackets with kinky plaited hair & that
overwhelming little space between their front teeth
smooth stockings & legs   Spanish sexiness   men in
muted Italian undershirts   tan & muscular   sun glinting
off tiny gold crosses on Tundra chests   off window tiles
& exquisite cornice
                        OH
                           I could learn to speak Spanish
if the weather stayed nice   & the Puerto Ricans
didn't grab for my tits   I could take in subtle idioms
and conversational twitches   and eavesdrop whole
sentences into my vocabulary   I could be wonderful
& translate Lorca and Raquel Jodorowsky   Go
to South America finally & live in Lima and the burning
agate winds of Peru, purified on the dry sun-seared slopes,
skies as intentional as the blue dyes of Morocco, air so
real it moves among the clouds like a benevolent giant!
I will sit there at the cave entrance laughing in the light
& sticking pins into an adobe image of my high school
Spanish teacher, rolling my r's at the heavens, smoking
yerba buena   or whatever it is they do

            O Maté   Maté!
I have painted the map of South América on my bed   & I
sleep in the high fantastic mountains of Peru!

     even now in the provinces   the truck drivers
are keeping their eyes out for me.
I could never make a mistake in Spain or Portugal
they would lean from their cabs   right through town
there must be a road we could take together
along the Rio Guadiana   The Olives!   The
Iron   the thousands of sheep   bumping in our
dusty sunlight   peace comes to me at such times
& Europe will never be complete without me anyway
I could run into you on a street in Malaga
and not make a fool of myself   I'm sure of it!
How can the classic pose of centuries fail?
Everyone knows—   even now as the demonstration
passes between the barricades   construction workers
point at me   That girl   they say
That girl   she should be in Spain!

We go out to fly the kites. Where is the wind
that we need?   I lift the great ruby-eyed bat kite
&   the little striped fish from the Orient   &
we run!   over the grassy strip
tiny stars jump from the knees of our dark corduroy
in bracing ochre air the kite goes up   & comes down
the children shout & cheer   we do it again & again!
I am thinking of my cheek in the soft flesh of
your shoulder. I am thinking of Afghanistan!   lips
of the fierce mountain fighters
The dust of Khyber pass   on my silver toe ring
Our long limbs resting against denuded cliff   tan
& gleaming   I will borrow N's pack   and
handy Coleman   will you trust me   just once more?

Passports drop from ornate rooftop molding
stone drapery for the gala reception.   Architecture
filling up the space
                              & Edifice
      Raised ornaments who are a part of looking up
Here I am!   across the street   A gaudy parallel of
your white tiles   but both shining   in the clear
   for one more afternoon.

Yes I got the card from Spain with the little
donkey and the oranges
and the one with the translucent waters of the
blue gulf sparkling in the sun
tips of the submerged cliff coming through like
miniature craggy islands above the glimmering golden sand.
I put on the little rose carved from the angel skin coral,
my sandals slapping the dusty marble steps
and I think of you   climbing the Tuscan hills
as I go down to get the mail.
R sends me the Blue Mosque at sunset
just last week D sent me an interior of the same building.
I often have a mad desire to pee on the floor of such
places. I don't know what it is   Something
wrong with me I suppose . . . . . .   I suppose you can
catch a glimpse of vineyards and stone barns from
the three-room villa   It's still spring
here in New York   everyone is out   on the stoops
& in the street   flaunting their haughty charms
Yesterday in the park the children built a sand castle
medieval with crenelated walls   like the Chateau de Marcues
you saw   on the road to Biarritz,   overlooking the lovely
Lot River Valley   and near the prehistoric caves of
Lascaux!   and last night M asked Patrick   if he knew
where babies came from   and Patrick answered   "Paris!"

I keep the souvenirs you sent from Panama
in the little jeweled box you sent from Morocco
But I want to be a foreigner too   a stranger
in a strange land   To sit down on the Himalayas
and decide   between Nepal & China
toss pebbles into the lakes on the Tibetan Plateau
wiggle my toes in the freezing water
I'm not an idiot   I know what I want!
Citizens go down the street costumes all aflutter
they don't imagine me where I'm really at
blasted on the earth's highest peak
mountain villages and paths fainting brilliantly
at my feet
O My Heart that flies from the window   into
the marvelous night   Sublime!
and ridiculous in the giddy altitude
No one from the Embassy would recognize me now
no one from the little bodega
As though I were a masterpiece   the snow
falling on my lashes

england and scotland are the paradise of walkers.
Thomas Grey himself walked the Lake Country in 1769
and after a long day's tramp found the inn's best
bedroom damp and dark and so went flamboyantly on
for another 14 miles to Kendal and an inn with a dry bed
O Thomas Grey I would have come too
through 14 miles of blushing crepuscular forest   and Europe
under my feet at last   I even skip the
pastoral beauty unbound   the sound of all those waterfalls
the sparkling lakes that turn completely black when the
long shadows of the mountains throw themselves down
I don't even mention at all the fresh trout   and partridge
the oaten cakes young mutton and the good country-brewed ale
I don't rave on about the Druid circles of stone
the serene villages!
is it so much to ask   Europe and a dry bed!

A slight drizzle falls on the Ethiopian bracelet
on my arm   wet leaves stick to my ankles
water drips through my matted curls   The sheep
of the Caracul Mountains of Afghanistan have such
woolly ringlets   you said
How can you stand in thigh deep sweet clover
and not speak to me now!
Like a heartbreaking still from an Ozu film
under your wide black umbrella   or an afternoon when
everyone speaks of trivialities and a hideous
tension mounts,   You have manufactured
the perfect silence   into which   we cannot even breathe
a Great Circumstance   from a little event
OH porch swing and juniper   and woodpile   and rusty pump,
where is the wild and careless?   the joy inexhaustible!
the journey to the Crimea?   the stunned snow of the
frozen Finnish Gulf!

I climb into bed and roll towards the window
my brother's on a Swedish ship in the Panama Canal
heading out towards Amsterdam and Hamburg
I'm lying here looking up   at 2 million Minnesota stars
moonlight   some figured brocade trailing over
Canadian Thistle and Common Dandelion   over Blue Verain
and the catnip by the screendoor with the ivy
Burdock under the apple trees   Pennsylvania Smartweed
down by the creek   and Spiny-leaved Sow-Thistle
in the ditch   The windows here
unlike those of a charming Venetian Palace
don't overlook a canal   no colored panes
Nevertheless   it's Dazzling
the moon blooms on car door   and chrome
on granary roof   and along the curled tin
of the drain pipe under this dormer
luminous blond tongues   and perfumes of red clover
phosphorous angles light up the yard   the driveway
the fence   the tops of the corn stalks
I bury my face in those fiery gestures!   the rustling
silk of that sky!

Everybody in Granada is probably asleep anyway.

I go up on the roof of the half-collapsed barn
A Hamm's in my hand   a suntan on my mind.
Over the protruding shingle nails   the broken beams
the splintered rafters   come small hands with saws
and hammers
we're going to build a clubhouse up here! they say
and build and bang and cover me with wood chips
clouds burst into white lace flowers
sawdust floats in the hot still air
some bridges are going up beside the club-house
the noise becomes tremendous
Well   I've seen America first
and now I'd like to try some airplanes, yachts,
and fast European cars   private Lear jets and
Ferraris   the sapphire waters off St. Lucia
some nice peaceful jaguar shooting in Mexico
the black volcanic sands of St. Vincent
I'd like to show this shocking pink bikini
    the lavender shores of the Mediterranean.

Coming home this morning   wearing last night's velvet
& the opal-studded jacket   the lovely pink feathers
brushing my cheek   askew
across Amsterdam on the dangerously high platform heels
silvery sidewalks   then stones and sand
grinning construction workers stand around on
and make me blush for my uncombed frizzy hair
my sleepy eyes   my tottering stride   your smell
rising from me   a dark throbbing perfume bazaar

Ah! If only one could see the Baltic from here
the soft & wispy fogs
Now is the time to be glamourous and well-traveled
To pause on the vermilion terrace   & shake my tousled locks
my earrings   and my brooches   over the ancient
Mogul tiles   perfect symmetries in oblong
and rectangle
             the whitest sand and the whitest dunes!
the public baths below me on the street   vapors curling
in the dust   at the base of the flowering almond trees
like a sun-drenched brawl.
In freezing and scorching regions and in a bedroom
decked with irises   with all the increasing and wild
speed of success   fluttering through the construction dust
a woman made without past or history   in love
but never in Europe!

Kicking the step   with the top of my wet tennis shoe
I thought   OH   I'll never get to college   or even
to Mexico   where everyone has been
including the sturdy TARHETA POSTAL in my pocket
Sandy has written on the back   "I don't like washing
and cooking all day"   and on the front
the Nayar Mountains form a radiant green blur
over the shoulders of two "Natives of the Nayar Mountains"
colorful mantles held on with safety pins   the one
on the left clutching a midget-sized fiddle   *Here*
is the victory   of those   whose hearts break
over the spaghetti   forever leaving the table
and returning   as though nothing has happened.

              To demand a front row seat!
the waves on an embroidered dress   in the heart of China
where lines of outdoor toilets define the angles of the road
& tufts of hair stand up like promise on the heads
of the populace.   I want to lose control
the way I used to   throwing my arms around him
madly kissing his vest and lapels   a straining ever upward
caught in that intensity of humiliation   risking everything
again   for one sign of love   one step
into that future I am proclaiming   Oh balmy
breezes   blowing dirt into my face   Oh herbal medicine!
I have seen a picture of the Wild Goose Pagoda.

The emperor sulks in his pavilion
he is not accustomed to this glaucous light
paradisiacal darkening that will soon be rain
& I sulk   on the pine bench   beside you
I want the beginning back again
These volumes of self improvement have done me no good
I want the auspicious beginnings   the first glances
the first trembling fingers on my lips   and
pressing the flimsy curls wetly against my neck   over and
over and over again   Puppy Love!   High School Romance!
   oh so delicious   to be wanted that way
when every time you saw me you got a hard-on.

           human nature lets go too soon
I don't want to be your first casual relationship!
transported alone to the frantic lush of Nepal
the Great Sad bushes   and their vegetative wisdom.
I would squat down there with a heavy heart
I would fall back   I would lose everyone
                                 under a cloudy sky.
Now, through the flaming saffron turban on the postcard
I understand the meaning of the art of travel
Just as Chang Hsu understood calligraphy while hearing
the music of a street band   and the wine-loving monk
Huai-su while watching the wind blow summer clouds
     You see   I know   I Know
        we have all been somewhere
Yet the emperor is sulking in his pavilion
                               & he has Everything!
and all my life I've answered "a little"
when what I really meant was "a lot."

a blond kid goes by   driving a load of oats to town
he is the scornful young Andalusian
amorous   & grubby
                                        why is it frivolous
to want to see   the dark swans of Tanzania
the children might feed them water plants   & I
could sun my ankles on the charmless cement border
of the pond   Sweet dissolution of my fantasies
I scoff at the rashness of the Habitat
We would sleep together among the goat tracks
                              Exposed to a real life.
Removed from the centerfold of your imagination
I will be able to distinguish myself   a facet
of the Great MidWest   strong & sensible
a girl who can follow the moon right down the middle
of a gravel road.
                         A monument of the Pioneer Spirit
          I was born here   in the land of sky blue waters
                                        just like Hamm's Beer

Beyond them the sunlight on the gravel was stunning
the sweltering heat dashed upon the lilies
the Hibiscus bloomed   and wilted 2 hours later
I won't explain my actions there

   O Rustic Hymn
       I know what it is   to lie awake all night
without even being able to take yourself seriously.
Still gaga   from the flourishes of the day . . . .

He erected cairns to mark the tail   I scooped
dry earthstars into my pockets   and mailed them away
to you.   He had entered his element   Light
leaked between the trees to guide him
We joked a lot   the Yellow-Billed Cuckoo
flew from the Mexican Juniper to a nearby thicket
damsel flies balanced on the toes of our shoes   idyllic
& heraldic   like turquoise   like the ruins of Tiffauges

At the evening dishes   in front of the sink
I was buying maps of the Syrian desert   where the
hills are sand-colored
    just to glimpse   your camel's feet

      Blue Ash   and Ashleaf Maple

                big chunks of blinding cotton clouds
space   and everytime I saw the hawk
         I didn't have the binoculars with me
I wasn't sure if it was Gray Goldenrod   or Pine-Barren
I never really knew what the bird with the yellow front was
it lacked the black V of a Meadowlark   I am convinced
that the growth I thought was Catnip   was   in fact
catnip   despite the arguments of outsiders
The Mimosa did not have thorns   and as far as I could tell
it looked exactly like the Albizzia.   Maybe
those were Shining Willows growing in the marsh
maybe Bayleaf?   & the stately somber
poplars were probably cottonwood   but
even allowing for the fatigue, the encroaching darkness,
and the excitement of the children   it was a Horned Owl.
In spite of numerous efforts I failed to locate the cat
that yowled all night and vanished during the day
were all the elms   American Elm   frankly, who knows!
was the brown bird with the popsicle-orange belly
a female Baltimore Oriole   if so where was her mate?
For God's sake what were those birds in the flock that
flew over us at the cemetery that afternoon   Red heads
with a black body?   Most of the gulls were
Franklin's Gull   the "Prairie Dove" of the Great Plains
but   in truth a large number were not   though
they may have been in the process of seasonal color change—
it was just not possible to get excited about those few
the majority were so perfectly marked!   on second thought
none of the swallows were Bank   all of them were Barn and
Tree Swallows
  they stood on the wire
    ridiculously tiny passengers on transatlantic steamers
          arched over the railings . . . .

Dotty lay figures on postcards   lacking individuality
poised on foreign hillsides   at least they have gone somewhere
and had time to sit down   A rosy wash
the shade of ripening apples   floods their temples
Thanks for the Rugged Grandeur of Glen Coe   & the
lapland tundra under the midnight sun.
Tragedy requires emotion   and across the courtyard
a Latin woman screams and screams   she is lost   in the Andes
in the Black Forest   weeping at the foot of the Pyrenees
for her there are no others   the scene is desolate
the man has arranged his head at an oblique angle to his
right shoulder   strollers are trying to calm her.   For me
it's a long story of desertions and abandonments
Time spend staring at the backs of doors   or a
vanishing miniature on a path   Someone seen from an opposite
sidewalk   or a sprinting athlete   admired   from a
fourth floor window.   All nearness banned by his plans   for
the Absolute   the Ideal
trafficking in that anguish   I am stirred forever
by the proximity   of the border!
when I throw the coins   they say   it furthers one to have
somewhere to go   I cannot be the angel in the doorway
the patient town   one returns to   after having lived a full life
In short   I will not wait here for you   Suckered
by a brush with perfection   Germany has famous
walking tours in the Bavarian Alps   beyond that
towards Sweden's border   are Norway's mountains

POSTCARD

        The cyclist from Bologna
        stands to the right of his cycle
        his moustache is so large
        I thought he was holding a taco
        in his teeth.

She had ruby red lacquer on her fingernails
sprinkled with gold glitter
elbow to wrist tin bracelets
a skinny shimmy-down   baby blue gown
of velvet portiere with peaked shoulders
trimmed in squirrel
gilded thongs crisscrossed around each lavender ankle
Her hair in the numerous tight braids
Of the Saharan girls   hung with
dried seeds and etched copper ornaments
with impeccable minute triangular boxes   engraved
and stained   hinges like the jaws
of some marvelous microscopic fish
under a broad-brimmed European hat   of
beaded Zulu designs   A plump skin pouch
A piece of flawless quartz at her throat
She was at least six feet tall strapped on her platforms
standing on the corner of 108th St.
in front of a heavenly azure wall   with a cloud sign
saying   **PARIS BLUES**

"*He* flys to Bangkok every now and then   just to jack off"
and a flattened thatched cottage arrives in the mail
with a message from M.
I was leaning on the glass display case at the party   and
someone said   "The islands"   but I was looking for him
thinking as usual   "HA! He hasn't seen anything yet."
Trying to appear less desperate than before   throwing myself
forward into the noise   the thumb-sized rose at my navel
blushing soft petals of unnamable tortures and fevers
But not unhappy
a person in such a state can be perfectly happy!
someone who realizes their own hysterical clumsiness
is a person in control of herself.
O my arm that traps your hair against the pillow
my elbow in your shoulder   my knee in your groin
the night you called from the bed— "See if you can
raise the window-shade without putting your foot through
my guitar and knocking over all the plants."
What a destiny   to be the inexperienced actor in Agamemnon
who, whenever he moved his head, caused clouds of powder
to rise from his hair   because
in the 1st act some foot powder had accidentally been spilled
on his head
So past personal history puffs over us and identifies
outrageous failings   we work so hard to put them all behind
When I had finished all the tasks he simply
found more for me to do   the pressure remained
at a constant level   While pucks of rain hit the windows
saying, "Cairo"   "Cairo"   "Cairo"

44

Can I be on the street again!   a lost soul again
dispatched igneous into the day   with burning cheeks
Buffeted about by your fascination of the traditional
"girlie" figure in silk   O give it up!   give it up
the scarf drops from the firm curve of the neck
the voile blouse faints under the jonquils
Husky bilingual adolescents bash by us   on our way
these are the shoes and waistlines of a people
of a nation!   tough tight jeans and mascara
passing POPO'S and MARY'S
My ears awash in your ideas of perfection   I fling myself
towards them   the way one builds a table   in order
to forget the state of the world   the way
N's mother must have clung to the frozen log
when she realized the bonfires between the thick trees
were in pairs and all at the same level   and that
she was surrounded by a pack of wolves.
The best is often so removed it's like a picture
one can only stare at   dumbfounded
Collapsing across the pillows   Him in Kiev   in Moscow
in Siberia   the white snow drifting   his blue eyes . . .
     The cold gleam of the icicles drives me nuts!
I should go along   make bear skins into coats for him
Russia!   Poland   Caracas
Hokaido!
          I don't want to know what's wrong with me!

               Argentina,
                    I'll come down   curl up
with the South American Owl Monkey
watch his enormous eyes   all through the night.

tightly woven fibers of virtually anything that
could be woven into fabric   flax, linen, or
cotton
                    The Sail
for as long as man has braved the sea   he
has relied upon the force of the wind   to move his vessels.
Sails of Rotterdam   sails hung from the masts   asleep
& dreaming of the Indies   anchored
at the doors of houses   Sails that have captured the wind
& the Nordic trade   I have waited for sails
Presenting myself to the sea like a stupendous fjord
I have reduced myself to a brush for the deck
lowered myself to the most ignominious extreme
assumed the look of one so abject   the foggy canals
offered themselves   as a promise of something better.
I pulled rejected animals from the drowning murk and
slime and they followed me home   immediately resuming
the heinous personalities that had caused someone
to chuck them into the canal in the first place.
I surrounded myself with these lives that hated the world.
We gathered in the lichen and fungi, liverwort and fern,
on the broken vegetation   that adjoined the cement boundary
of the canal   and wept drearily into the fog
bonded by a lover's rejection and common misery
we knew what hard luck was   & I think we made the most of it
we dragged back and forth along the grey wall
waiting for sails   in an artistic pose . . . .

Now   here is a shirt   sewn from Old Sails
patched and mildewed, weathered and stained
Sturdy sails   prized possession of the sailors
authentic old sails   changing tack on the open sea!

My mother has given me this shirt made from Old Sails
&   I have put it on.

O thick Egyptian jungle
    O sodden lilacs of my youth
  & the waters that brought us together!

FROM *a brass choir approaches the burial ground* (1977)

or

"from the arms of one man
into the arms of another."

"In view of the human condition,
the only sustainable posture is one of humor."
— Pirandello

I walk into doors   to everyone's delight
I constantly step on the toes of those I happily kiss
   I smash into strangers while shaking hands
I wrap my arm around the dark lamp-post   putting on
my coat in the rain
  I drop all the papers I'm holding
    I trip on the rug
I slip on the waxed floor   on my way to the door
ruining a graceful good-bye   only the whippet
understands me   only the parrot   and maybe
the comet   who knows what it means
to be perfectly in orbit   and still crack up
just because something gets in your way   just because
something else   didn't know you were coming
forgot to move   or couldn't   and there you were
spinning around each other for a moment   then
flung out again   quite breathless and puzzled
into that silent icy realm   between the outer edges
of the solar system   and the nearest stars
where it is never 10:30   or noisy city   or mid December
when   we see you O Kohoutek   whose head is really
in the clouds   huge ones of hydrogen atoms
containing the mysterious source molecule
I have the same problem   I can't really see where I'm
going either   and yet a tremendous force is shooting
me forward at terrifying speed.
sequins   and opals taunt the regular dark
radiation pressure buckles the tail away from the sun
into telescopes   and notebooks   Schmidt camera   and
scientific data   a gorgeous answer
some think comets the last chance   to find primordial material
to know who   or what   peered up from the fire and grunted
last time   you came by   10,000 years   or so   ago
nameless   & nonchalant
with your secret of inner economy   & longevity

we are desperately roaming the streets for such things!
and some   bored by it all
          like the man on my bed
languishing   telling me   everything bores him
       Get a telescope   I want to tell him   I just want
to scream   Get a telescope!

LOVE SONG FOR T.

        The moss makes soft green bumps along the shore
        like when I had hives on my butt
        soft pink slightly raised circles
        and the doctor said   "Looks like an allergy,
        go home and sit down and try to think of all
        the new things that have come into your life
        in the last few days,   you're probably allergic
        to one of them"   and it was the day after the
        first afternoon I had made love with you
        & I thought   Oh No!

WHO NEEDS IT

    the skaters dodge   the way   you lie across the ice
      Down again!   Most friends will dodge you too
    noting only the color of your sweater   the
    amazing sheen of your frozen gloves   as they
    glide past   netting blue   & silver light.
    It is equivalent to the feeling   things aren't
    going to go the way you planned.   He has handed
    you a slip of paper   on which   nothing is written
    yet it says   "At a certain age
    you will toss your morals to the wind"
    Oh Daphne
        who refused love from the start
    I too want to be done with the folly of beginning!
    We clapped and clapped when the terrible singer had finished
    so relieved   it was over   we rose to our feet and descended
    Only those trying to impress their escorts were smiling.
    There are others with such irreversible clarity   that
    lying beside you at night   they will simply say —
    Please take your elbow out of my eye — or will remain
    full length   on your bed watching you   Rebuff
    to answer anything
               Sobriety that chokes the heart!
    One would have better luck speaking to a landscape.
    because of this   my life has been
    The Soggy Pillow Testimony.
    When Hemingway shouted up "What am I going to do? I
    have no typewriter!"
    Dorothy Parker leaned over the rail of the Rotterdam
    and threw down the brand new portable she had bought
    to use on the voyage.   Had it been me
    I would have shouted back   "Sell some of your fishing tackle!
    . . . . . Ernest"
    I can get dressed by myself
    I know which way is North
    Even without Nietzsche, Milton, or Wittgenstein

I know enough to ask   Where is the gate   to paradise?
I can walk
I can answer
I can bend
with the one   who ties his sneakers   & says
         "I'm leaving this circus"

HOW TO GET BY

I often wonder
just to get your attention
I am usually indifferent to what I tell you,
scarcely endangered by hysteria
I remain on the coast
& never go out further than where I can stand up.
The lazy valley is destroyed every afternoon
promptly at 4
after that we have tea
& go to the volcano at 6.
Myself, I enjoy seeing deserts being made
& I try to be there at 8 every Tuesday.
Children seem to like watching the mountains
forming
and are often dazzled as we trace a river
to its first raindrop.
I remember having to diagram a rainbow in
the sixth grade — it left me limp for hours.
Also I received particularly high marks
during the term on thunderstorms
(& here is where the girls excel —
the boys being better at dissecting clouds).
But, looking back, it's the words of a bent
hooded old matron that I've come to depend
most upon
"My dear," she rasped, resting her shoulder
on the wall of the cave where we were observing
the development of stalactites, "My dear, sweet
almond oil, oil-of-rosemary, & two drams of
cocoa oil massaged gently into the underarms
& insteps will carry you through
almost
any situation."

Go ahead   Spit the mushrooms   I cooked so perfectly
back into your plate   mumbling something about
   sand   See if I care!   Outside that door
an entire segment of history is waiting to treasure me
I'm fated to be rich and spoiled   pampered by millions!
Wafting towards breakfast   under globs of crystal   and
gold leaf   my trains of snowy chiffon and dotted swiss
bounce off the marble columns   breathless
and outrageous   even in the rain
          even with my satin slippers soaked!
Through halls so oceanic   the Arabic and Persian rugs
form archipelagos
                against the walnut knobs of the velveteen
loveseat   against wicker settee
& the drawing room chair with the great swollen rose
painted on cretonne

                    Crush these flowers for my sunken bath!
                              and listen
                 you can hear
colossal foamy gardens squeezing up
between the toes of the serpentine goddesses

The all-night dancers still reflected in the pool
onlookers swathed in discarded fruit rinds
curtains drifting out over the goldfish . . . .

One flitting afternoon you might stand
cooking your own mushrooms   realizing   "What a blunder!"
to have lost her   to the pearls   and the polo ponies

   Pin stripes and pastels   linen and lavender silk
                    O Pardon my Snobbery!
                        my Rapture
                           my weeping!   into the

                              imported folds of this pink shirt
while palominos gallup through sprinklers on private grass
& under gaudy yachts   white birds have surfaced   like these
Damned mushrooms   on the sea!

FANTASY 22

      O to be young & neglected!   Left alone for long
      unguarded hours in the ruined palace.   The delicious
      yield of the marvelous rugs and tapestries!   To roll
      with wild abandon   down flights of smooth cool marble
      stairs   & get up   bruised & tortured by love!
      exhausted in the tangled garden   overgrown
      exotic shrubbery stinging your thighs & shoulders.
      To leap   into icy waters of bronze fountains   & gasp
      for breath.   Here are diamonds that shatter on your hair.
      & the thick wings of the peacocks.   Loose trousers
      of the night, dark purple that billow & fold with a
      shudder.   I sat beside you on the bed   my senses
      reeling.   Forehead pressed through torn silver lamé
      to lean on a clear cold window   The palace hounds
      withdraw along velvet corridors   & now to follow them!
      To fling from balconies   into enchanted
                                                          rosewood drawing rooms
      To swoon!   To drop   upon mauve servants in
      immaculate dress.   To slide your ear along Persian
      silk divan   & insist on silence!   O to be young &
      neglected   Left alone for long unguarded hours
      in the ruined palace!

UP IN THE AIR

        Look through these binoculars
        & you will see
        that the children have painted tiny gardens
        on the end of each lens
        & that through this washy greenery
        Antonin Artaud runs screaming
        "Motorhead!   Motorhead!"
        flinging out from his brow
                      droplets of mercury
        little balls like the disconnected bellies of
        fat dwarfs
                forming hexagrams at his feet.
        The Great Northern Elk & the Caribou
        obscured slightly by the lush outcroppings
        are entranced by Artaud
        he deciphers the lines for them
        they graze and nod from time to time

                I am only mentioning this to remind you
                how it is.
You will only find wonder in the first encounter
after that a vast indifference & then
finally
friendship
But what a hoax!
A smile circling the bone your teeth are busy on.
Standing in the doorway dressed for skiing
Applying these moments to your life.

"WANTING YOU"

While you were going   up the hill   in the
stunning snow   the dazzling crystals that
floated & fell   in the streetlights
Snug inside your black 1930s coat,   images
of your   "Goodbye"   "Goodbye"   rehearsed vivaciously
in my mind   a sudden cynosure where my attention
knelt in rapt admiration   So mad with love!
So frantic with desire!   Again and again I watch
you turn before me   That slightly inclining
three-quarter turn   Your gloved hand poised
the overwhelming irresponsible joy of your voice
as it stepped into the gay Russian Troika   the
stamping   steaming horses!   the gold & blue banners!
My heart left me then   tumbling & splashing up
the hill   the snow melting where it touched

Waking up alone   I explode from the bed
nervous & shaking   in this steamy room
Is is these moments that have led me here
this need I have to sleep beside you .
that has caused all the trouble in my life.

When you're down and under and crushed and shattered
smashed and trodden and beaten, bamboozled, kicked and
destroyed   lost out, gone mad, fell back, shot up,
done in, wiped out   When your heart is broken   and
your nose is running, your days are numbered, your lot
is cast, you're wasted, worried, choked up and ruined
left out, disinherited, sweating, frustrated, alone and
demolished, hopeless, despairing, depressed and insane
you're lousy   you know it   you wish you could change
Your coat's ripped, your nose is crooked, your brain is
mush, your hands are cursed, your life is worthless
and you're uncomfortable   a hunchback, a sucker,
a recluse, a frog   When you know you can't make it
You're hideous, helpless, pusillanimous, squirrelly and
dumb

      just bear in mind
     that 9/10's of everything
       is posture

      Stand Up!

TRAVELING

　　　　I left it.
　　　　That was my burst of exuberance for the
　　　　entire stay.
　　　　The letters that followed were dug up
　　　　out of a box in the attic
　　　　events had gone by obvious to no one
　　　　　　　　　　　　　Subtle mechanisms
　　　　slick as otters under water
　　　　　　　　　　　　　　　a man
　　　　taking you out of joy　&
　　　　　　　　　　　　　into your clothes
　　　　　for the sake of it
　　　　a last resort
　　　　when you run out of sexuality on the open road.

　　　　Random productions begin sticking to every bush
　　　　& passing truck
　　　　　　　　　　we became the universe's reaction
　　　　　　　　　　to Itself.
　　annoyed
　　　　　　hassled
　　　　　　How awful!
　　　　　　　　　　in terms of tragic endearment
　　　　　we were accustomed to the original
　　　　& now this
　　　　　　　　these repetitious cities
　　　　　　　at the peak of attention
　　　　　　　　　　　modern miracles
　　　　　　　at ease with time.

THANK YOU, AMERICA

       And   Oh Wheaton!
                        for your shirtless hot youths!
   intoxicating chests buffeted by the breeze
in the rolled-up sleeves of their faded levis
      terrific muscles under their open shirts
I could smother in caresses   a posture
just between the cab of Dodge pickup   and
the gravel drive
standing on the springboard of a red grain truck
tan-armed hand on the rolled-down window rim
I weep on the dashboard   kissing those locks of hair
Hugging the necks of that wild shyness
Where is the applause of a crowd of enthusiasts
for a jaunty torso   barely inclining forward
sliding from the seat   I press to my eyes the image
OH Moocher of my peace   A body slightly in the air
halfway to the ground
all bravura and boldness   before the grain elevators
Armfuls of sky!   Heavy dark boots and light tousled hair

             Such beauty rips me limb from limb!

     I'm not a crazed sex maniac   it's anatomy
these supple joints   the sporting step   that takes them
dazzling blond hair brushing their shoulders
blue eyes dashing forward
      bounding up the feverish drowsy streets of
     Wheaton, Minn. pop. 2,209   Right past me
   sitting here   the hottest blow job in town!

the great Yu of the Shia Dynasty before
he became emperor he was the minister in
charge of flood control . . . .

       Be careful not to say too quickly   "He's putty in my hands"
       or   you may appear in midnight downpour   digging a trench
       in frozen ground   half an acre of melting snow around your
       ankles   & Tired   of being that Scorched Romantic figure
       smoldering in drowned weather   of ruined exhausted charm
       & feverish   sick of the soppy rayon of the theme!
       a story so complicated it can only be told in 83 episodes
       Once I was on the phone   and then face to face
       both equally disastrous   he did not even have the decency
       to stamp his foot   when he said   "You sat on your ass."
       it was like finding yourself still reading a story
       you could tell from the first page   wasn't going to be
       worth it.   He actually said "You have no rights
       Moral Law alone makes you my prisoner
                      Your Karma will get you . . . "
          a dangerous pause   "think about it"

       No!   I refuse to be the one responsible for everything
               the Japanese Plum blossoms in severe cold
               and through all this my mission remains clear

                   I am the Tooth Fairy!
         embodying that accepted logic   that will give me magic power
           to trade silver for enamel   and still come out ahead

       "What an excellent thing it is," Confucius said,
       "to be able to find a source of consolation in yourself!"

"Where there's writing, there's hope" She
once told me crossing a street

        Just because the sea is calm   doesn't mean that
        I can drop you   at the airport   with a cheerful kiss
        calling out   "See you in five days"
                                        Thanks to you
        I now can tell   the song sparrow   the white throat   and the
        chipping sparrow   apart   & be happy   just to
        crouch   with one foot   in the chilly swamp   a
        shivering arabesque   in darker night   folded
        fingers poised on flashlight switches   Desiring
        only a view of some frog's head   as it
        emerges from oozing tufts   Singing the song
        that brought us here
                                  toot!   toot!
        three dozen throats   we can't see   a chorus
        of tin whistles   as invisible   as hocus pocus &
        the famous Silver Sign the constellations hold
                All Is Not Lost!   it reads
        Does Nature really know something we don't?
        In Japan there is a mountain   named Monkey Mountain
        but there are no monkeys on it   long ago
        there were thousands   however, civilization advanced
        and the monkeys fled   Now tourists read the placard
        Monkey Mountain   & stand squinting into the trees
        gesturing   without the slightest reservation . . . .
           With him my love just flew out the window   he didn't
           bother to look up as it went by.   Desperation!
        that made me too serious for my own good.   Even the Jesuit
        grinned, "You get 20, 25 priests holding confession   it
        just goes like nothing."
                Crazy icy night, that goes by talking to itself
            "You Bum!   You leave us high and dry   and call that

information!"   Once I had nothing   now so much is
at stake   my teeth are chattering   & I had wanted to
grow up calm and lyrical   like the sea
on our way to the airport

            O Sunday water   in this big dish!

"She's a real tough cookie" — Susan Howe

"He has a stick up his ass"   You put it so well!   Overwhelmed
by his charm, arrogance, eloquent taste, and brilliance   I had
not recognized the rigid back   the myopic courtesy. At the opening
ignoring the fact that I was holding a drink in my hand   he
continued to shake it   sloshing wine all over ourselves and the
small crowd that was gathering.   A dizzy vapor
shifts across the Spartina Patens   sulphur-colored grasses hide
the tidal flats   the gull shakes his head to get rid of the brine
and what I do is functional too!
                            I am no lonesome decoration on the shore
noticed only in the absence of others!   A friend who was so tough
she simply said of the poor old professor in the ballet   "He shoulda
got one while he was young"   That same girl seated   balanced
on a thin rail   holds over her head a leafy branch from one of the
shade trees   to ward off the advancing rain. She is tilted slightly
backward
as though extending a hand to fend off blows of heavenly retribution.
Another   darker woman   crouches on 31st and Broadway   modestly taking
a sponge bath   while early morning crowds pour by.   Dipping a rag
into a battered tomato tin filled with water   she discreetly lifts the green
frock away from her body with one hand   and washes with the
other
"We must not weep so that we may not be comforted" wrote Simone Weil
— There are ways of making the worst suffering bearable —   Absent
one leg Sarah Bernhardt went on acting. P.T. Barnum offered her
$10,000 for the amputated limb   and the right to exhibit it.

             O Alkaline sap of the Ash
gone blue in autumn   purple in tone
Reddest Sweetgum   Sumac and dogwood   Oak &
Poplar Aplomb in birch and Scarlet.   Tulip tree
& Willow bright yellow   Beech   Mahogany   & Prune vermilion
O Racy Sassafras   Redbud Blueberry in flame with Rose
& Orange
              Bounce off these windshields   as we go
laying rubber past old high schools Yelling "Dactyls!
Sestina Iambic Pentameter!"   at the top of our lungs
   Crashing through drifts of Ginko leaves
There are times when you must throw yourself overboard
in order to survive

                 the salty tourmaline moon and the stars
                 they are lovely   and cannot be entered by reason
                 ....or .. rondel ....

YELLOW YO-YO'S

        For years I was an outlaw
        Wanted by the law in Frisco
        married to one man   living with another
        children it seemed   all over the place
        then I went straight
        Caesar & Brutes
        Anthony & Cleopatra
        Abbott & Costello
        Lewis & Clark
        Damon & Pythias
        Burns & Allen
                You & Me, Kid
              my angel in the morning
              I can hardly see for the golden
              feathers all over the bed

FROM *Hearts in Space (1980)*

> "I belong to a country I have abandoned."
> — Colette

. . . and I am reminded of Colette on the train
that morning asking herself   "If you have left
half of yourself behind, does that mean you have
lost 50% of your original value?"

Handscroll with ink and colours on silk . . . .

In plate 44 Su Wu and Li Ling are shown parting   I
cannot tell if it is Su Wu leaning on his staff   & Li Ling
with sword and top-knot decoration   or Li Ling in furlined
robes   & Su Wu   with straw tucked under his belt.
Both faces portray agony and hysteria.   They have been together
in captivity for 20 years. Now   Su is unable to persuade Li
to return home with him.   Both are drenched in grief.
Is it the fault of the emperor . . . . or the Hsiung-nu nomads . . . . .
The thick footwear bumpy with wadding   there is nothing in the
landscape to console them   no Brewer's Weeping Spruce or pine
not a single make of sparrow   the seals of later collectors
do not decorate the borders
      Only space   whole lives lived to embody one theme
    Leaping to adjust a bolt on the wagon tongue   while
his tractor continued on across the field riderless   breaking
his wife's arm haying   and her nose by accident   when he
playfully   bounced frozen cow pies off the side of the barn
seven stitches in his own skull from rising suddenly while still
underneath the massive combine   too dangerous to work with
friends terrified to help   smashed by swinging boards   ramming
trailers   Knocked from hay racks by the power of his bale toss.
    Rippy   backing over oil barrels!   Having made the choice
you simply live accordingly   Exterior
lid of a box   gold lacquer and lead adventurin lacquer
on black lacquered wood,
        the painter seeks the life
  of the bamboo   not the form.

"Dearest Bupple,
.... I have no opinions really."   *Jane Bowles*

       Cilla, Blue striped violets, Narcissus, Crocus, Forsythia,
a bush outside my window covered   with petite white petals
Just this morning as I lifted my head from the pillow   Patrick
was saying   "Houdini walked through a brick wall . . . everyday!"
              When you know you are in for it
not even statistics are a consolation.   Finally
on the eve of the ship's party   she was asked to sing
but they had run headlong into a terrible squall
the piano was tied to the stage to keep it from flying off   &
they gave her a rope to hold unto   so she wouldn't fall down.
                    Abandoned
      like Genet at the hands of the customs officials   who
welcomed him with so much attention   & then shoved him off.
Friends can't wait to tell you   What a Botch!
you've made of things   Wishy-washy   Spineless   Can't
make a decision   innocent mealy-head,
                    Don't you have any opinions?
they ask.   A man we never saw before comes by to tell us
our barn & property are worthless   He wouldn't even tear
the barn down for wood   he says   Also
the community is falling apart and the neighboring towns too
& he is appalled by it.   You'll notice the main beams are
completely rotted   and the roof   well   there simply is no roof!
It's so far gone!   He glances with disdain on the crumbling
stone wall . . . . In the vulnerable aftermath of dinner   She
has indicated the V of swords   a tremendous struggle
where we stand   exhausted   leaning on flexed & sagging knees
  while our enemies rush towards the edge of the card.
      Triumph   is relative   Lao Tzu warns from his cloud
"Success and failure are the same disease"   skinny
beard and robes   blown sideways by a continuous wind.

      After everyone died   his life began to take on the attributes

of a recluse   He would only go in to pick up his mail   every
two or three months, leave town with all the windows open,
letters swooping into wheat and rye fields
                    free samples bowling into the ditches.

"Some days," Dorothy Parker said, "it's better than
digging ditches."

for Rebecca Brown

The United States is giving the Suez Canal back to Panama
    it seems like only yesterday Tyrone Power was
building it   against all odds . . . . I thought
at dinner   When B said suddenly   "I hate my forehead!"
We all looked closer.   But no   it was a perfectly normal
forehead.   When Nijinsky died they cut open his feet
to see the magical bone structure   birdlike
though towards the last   he thought he was a horse
his legs under the loose   material   alluding
to a headlong gallop   away   from inner states of terror.
Jane Bowles in Paris   writing   "Dear Bupple . . . "   Telling
him   Alice Toklas admires your book tremendously   &
Eudora Welty came over to dinner   and is a great admirer
of yours . . .   As for her own work   Eudora had returned
the copy   unable to finish it   and a friend in the hotel
a charming   brilliant girl called Natika   didn't
like it either really   The days go by   they give us more
and more   and more to lose.   You lose!   This is not always
a tragedy.   Beyond a certain point   it is impossible
to live at face value   in the end it will be the length
of our extravagance   that allows us to imitate   at last
the masculine impatience!   The sea wedged like the chunk of
some jewel between the shore and the horizon.
Remember!   It was only the low houses that
made the men on horseback seem so important!   Without
passport, papers, or luggage   Refusing to turn back at
the border   we will merely say to the guards   "Let us Pass."
Greta Garbo made only 27 movies during her entire lifetime.
Beatrix Potter hated children.
Hawthorne wrote in his notebook: "Herman Melville's linen

is none too clean."
Or as She said   in a precocious letter shortly after the 2nd novel
"And to think of the Grande Affaire I gave up for it!   Lawdy!"

MONICA

My aunt   who died
at forty-two
had a little cabana
in the heel of each shoe

ODE TO ASEXUALITY

for J.D.

The second I get you on the couch   the kids come back
we missed the bus they say . . . .
     I must have eaten forty ears of corn   Enraptured
out of my mind!   there in the broomgrass   & Moonlight.
Drooling butter   Spilling salt   There was this marvelous
rhythm   He would say something   then I would say something
then he would say something   Who knows how much beer I drank   trying
to keep up with him.   If you could have seen   the night sky
A big pair of rhinestoned denims!   certain exceptional pinpoints
of light   that flew from,
                   The Hood!
of his car.   husks in flames   him on his elbow   & Silver
Silver! playing
             O Manic falsettos above the radio static!
          O Blazing Foreheads!
      O Simple!   Simple desires
              like the Great Bonfires of Europe!

As if   sexual fulfillment were a kind of Paradise!
That late hour in the dead of winter   when Clay threw his arms
around an entire length of stove pipe   & began to polka madly
with the section he had wrenched free.   Downstairs Bud awoke
to soot and ashes settling on his quilt   "Fire" he Yelled
into the thick hot smoke   taking the stairs three at a time   "Fire!"
"He thought that warm tin was a woman," Bud said, "I had to pry him
off of it."

              OH Pry Me Loose!

                                        I want
to roll   where dark sand blows in from Chasma Boreale   & all
across the 200 kilometer wide delta of continuous dunes   that
become irregular   and mottled to the south.

                                                                for Fanny

The baby bangs his forehead into the spoon.
          Usually I am speechless   struck dumb   encased
in silence
A mysterious light chafes the snow to rose   and
chapped silk
Terrible fires burn in the Hollywood Hills   Sissy
Spacek is interviewed   "The danger of fire   is just
something we have to live with here.   For years,"   she says
"I've made sure all the hangers in my closets   face
in the same direction."   The secret is knowing
                              Whether to laugh or to cry!
In the doorway   the young Indian   drunk   swaying   bent
double with laughter   choked   "Can you believe   at the
reservation   I was   the tribal counselor for problem drinkers!"
Or when   just home from the hospital   with
the newborn in her arms   she took a dizzy spell
at the top of the stairs   and toppled   head over
heels   the older children at the bottom   went
alternately mad with giggles   and wild with weeping
saw her coming   a billowing flannel nightgown   Flipping
now with a head   now without one   uttering AH   AH   and OOF.
M writes   I wait for someone to knock my broken heart
for a new loop
      K is certain that love is only a series of one night stands.
Don't talk to him on the phone, she said, it's bad enough
to talk to friends.
                  & yesterday at the doctor's office
a woman was saying to the receptionist   "The Christmas Specials
are so scary this year   made to frighten little
kids   tomorrow night they have the three wise men
landing   from another planet   What do they want to go and
ruin Christmas for . . . ."
                              Earlier I read a passage
            that seemed to suggest
            the beauty of balance
                        is   to fall over

for Kyran at 6 months

All That Glitters . . . .

       Here the picture is less gloomy.   Rumpled
sunrise on the snow   the baby wakes   and fills
the room with awkward battering
                  O Uncomplicated One!
       littlest fat face amid the sheets   a commotion
of arms   flapping   palest rouge of flippers crazily rowing
When I simply say   "Good Morning."   Who would have even
suggested   the shore life was trivial?   Last night
on the phone   I realized practically everyone is
a manic depressive   of sorts   With up   and down movements
Unlike the baby   who thinks he's a Trolley   singing Gong
Gong   Gong   He's testing his elbows   & humming.
Five minutes
into the chapter   I noticed that   males were
referred to as men   but females were referred to as wives
I remember blurting out at the party   "I have no father"
With a tremendous sense of relief!   From Grandmother   to
mother   I have passed down. Born of and through women alone.
We have   crawled under the barbed wire   & sat
on our own   sacred land!
                O Lug
                   little lug
                       & Oggie   when the wind
blows over the stubbles   it's Fall   meaning   some things
make themselves obvious by repetition.

        And
             Tu Fu!   Always shaking your head   when
you look my way   Don't give up on me!
             I know the moon bobs in the Great River's flow
             I know about Fame   & Office!
             I have taken   this moment   to celebrate leisure!
             To contemplate

              laziness   as a goal   And Schubert himself
who had a streak of it   an incurable sponge   But loved
by all   his friends   who were fiercely loyal
                                      & called him Tubby   He
was barely five feet tall   & a bloom   as from a Spanish balcony
                                    was in both his cheeks.

> "To be without humor is to be
> without intelligence."
>
> — *Tadeusz Kantor*

Kyran smashed a dozen eggs this morning   with
one quick yank of his baby wrist   he sent them all
flying   while I was speaking to him about   yogurt.   It's
another example of   Just because you're funny . . . .
. . doesn't mean you're joking.   Last week this perfectly
well-dressed businessman   carrying a briefcase   behind me
on the ramp at Grand Central   without warning
began unabashedly intoning   "Calling Green Lantern"
"Calling Green Lantern"   "Calling Green Lantern!"   George
Sand abandoned by her lover   wrote in her journal
"thank god I have heart disease!"   It is possible
to develop   permanent grooves   in the space   between
your eyes   without even realizing it's happening.   Ulysses
pointed out to me at dinner   "You're the only person I know
who frowns while they're eating."   All I know is   Once
Long Island was so dark   & had forests   Now when that hardy
group of locals   that literally break the ice   on the Sound   to
go sailing   held their annual   "Glug Party"   to elect a new "king"
A fight broke out   somehow   between the two top candidates
     — one the principal of the grade school here in town —
Details are lacking but   in the scuffle   the converted trophy was
demolished   the irate citizens   apparently bashing one another
over the head with it   during the fray.
                              Then
as though burlesque couldn't teach us all we need to know   we
are shown the tanks blotting the quiet asphalt swerve of the drive
the civilian prostrate   at the brink of the tip of the combat boot
the bulky khaki uniform of the guardsman   who as calmly as
picking his teeth   merely tilted the long weapon   & Fired.
the man on the ground jerked so   a squadron of gnats was flung up
from the garbage lining the streets   & it seemed loose petals
bolted from the mums   in the bottle   on the table.

                        Have you seen my heart?
                        who used to go out everyday
                        alone!
It was last glimpsed   riding   on a sleeve   a grove
of Beech trees in autumn depicted   mute grey & Palest orange
fleeing the 11 o'clock news!
                        The heart   tries so hard
to do some business
                    it sallies forth each day
                    into the voyage
                of Bill & Monty   two crumpled forms   rowing
                through hail & violent weather   emerging
                triumphant!   waving the mallards at B in his
                kitchen   who roared   "Jesus Christ! There's
                white caps on the toilet bowl   and you two
                are out on the lake   shooting ducks!"

GOODBYE SEPTEMBER

On Father's Day   she decided   it was time
to let him know he was going   to have a grandchild
her father was living on Hoyt St. then   optimistic
Bursting with the baby   She walked over   in
her maternity outfit   & presented herself.   He didn't say
anything   just sat staring at the TV.   He is such a
serious man,   she explained   never having read   what
Emily Dickinson wrote to Jane Humphrey in 1855   "Keep
a list of the conquests, Jennie, this is an enemy's Land!"
& caused the light to buckle   on the page.   These shreds of
yellow   crepe   A million hats   doffed towards   the mob
forming below   Fields strewn with scarlet regiments   who
only a few hours before   were writing in their journals while
they kept watch   uncontrollable   loving thoughts of the foe!
As though   russet scarves were dropping   & all   Hearts   going
down in flames!
                                                      Not all days
are like the afternoon you drove   the van   over your bicycle
Often what falls on our heads is subtler than leaves   &
in the tradition of that night   at the pool . . . . the violet
sky bunching   the bugs gathering around the flood lights
Our teeth and green faces under the darkening water   as more
& more bugs congregated   Humming
then collapsing   exhausted & dazed onto the pool   so that
whenever we surfaced   a veil of bug bodies   clung to our
eyelashes   & hair.   The attack takes place somewhere
in the vicinity of the chest.
    Has the victim been stricken by the view?
                                                                 Craning
there were times   I would have been content to see the name
of just one woman   on   the side of just one mailbox!
Instead   I drove listening   recalling how   hour after hour
they sat by the piano   going over & over the notes   the
songs   "There is a right way   to sing the blues," Ma
Rainey used to say   & then they'd take it   from
the top   Again!

>   For Beethoven who played the piano so badly . . .
>   but with such genius!

"Happy Mother's Day   To the Farm Girl Who
didn't go to college"   the inscription read   &
"from Pat."   Inside a glazed replica of a
Viking Ship   yellow oars springing from its sides
the deck   Dumb   regretting nothing   taking its signal
from   the sky   its orders from the light.   I
turn my ear   just so too   to catch the celestial guidance
the mysterious mumblings of fate   & hear
Not Li Po crossing the long range
Not Wang Wei murmuring amid the rushing grasses
But Connie   from Torch   selling me 4 more light bulbs!
    No protection against myself!   No University credentials!
    No lettered sweater!   No football scholarship to Ratcliff
    Yale   Bennington   Harvard   Sarah Lawrence   or
    Carnegie Tech.   No resumé   No translations!
    No manifesto!   No mastery of classical form or meter   &
    No possibility of ever abandoning them   to the horror
    of past scholarly   Outraged professors!
                                               But
I was born   the same year
Elizabeth Bishop met Pablo Neruda   in
Mexico   she'd seen him   on the airplane
wearing a dark   blue shirt   with small white anchors

POEM TO PISS EVERYONE OFF

I had the feeling early this summer of discovering
Gertrude Stein. I borrowed a copy of her selected
writings from Dick and retired here to read them.
I had this dazzling image of running through a wide empty
field towards her as she rose from a white rattan chair
during her garden tea. As I gradually drew within less
distance of her I felt some of my initial exuberance give
way & just as I came abreast of her I was stricken with
such overwhelming boredom that I instantly kicked her cane
out from under her and sped on by.

                                                for Emily (Dickinson)

The girl   working the xerox in the stationery store
has a "thing"   for one of the customers   "I'm in love!"
she blurts to complete strangers buying stamp pad ink.
"Am I shaking?   Last week when he came in   I
stapled my thumb."   It's not just a shift in season
but a hormone that sets the trees off too   from plain
green they go   cheeks flushed   & dropping
everything!
Like the baby bashing through them   hooting   "More!"
 &   the radio   announcing   "It's a Sealy Posturepedic morning!"
the landscape's gone silly   with abundance of motif   where
the tossed baby   Plunks   into the damp pyramid   &
is gone   From the base a small scuffed shoe
chanting   "Leafs!   Leafs!"   Here
is all the drama of the emperor's flight!   Imperial
dragon robes swept up   porcelains scattered
& the eerie glazed stillness   the soft mist Thudding
where the stately picnic   had been.
Is it a theory of numbers   or just   Quantity
that lifts us   up from under the armpits   with Fred
Astaire singing   in grand finale crescendo   "It
doesn't matter where you get it   as long as you got it!"

                         O furious Excesses!
She set her tough skiff   straightway
into the sea   for love of danger!
           tho all the birds have lost   their cover
                     & You   O Bald October
                            I knew you   when you
                            still had hair!

"I truly believe that we are enchanted," she said, "for this wood is not large enough for one to get lost in."

     The Haunted Pool —*George Sand*

  These are cotton woods.
  Fiddleheads scuff up in wool unspiraling
  It's thanks to Kenzo for these clouds &
  buttercups of crepe de chine go running down this slope
  all iridescent towards a figure sunk to the calves
  in sea As mysterious as The Magician who
  draped his cape over the volunteer Pronounced
  the magic words and then confidently thrust
  his sabre into the material
  An astounded & horrible cry burst from the cloth!
  In jail the magician was at a loss! Why had the man
  not disappeared! staring at the wall he went over &
  over the simple trick. Or the woman with two toddlers
  & her infant in her arms who came out of the shopping
  center sat the baby in its carseat on top of the car
  while she shoved the groceries in & arranged the other two
  children in their seats Then she got in &
  drove off. Barely a block away she was pulled over
  by a police siren getting out to speak to the officers She
  saw the baby precariously still balanced
  on the roof of the car. She said "I just forgot
  I had him . . . . "   We had started out
  on the yellow triangle trail then switched to the green
  circle trail then to the blue trail We may
  have traveled some distance on the orange and then taken
  the violet when we turned or the white We had crossed
  the plunging granite cliff and one of the horses had thrown
  a shoe before we became hopelessly lost.
  Crashing through Strangleweed, Wild Sarsaparilla, &
  Rattlesnake Fern flattened to the backs of the horses
  We scraped under the low branches Pushed
  through the thickets   Squashed by History

and immediate necessity   the afternoon I
descended from the gallery   Convinced   there was   A
Reason to live!   hit the street   & then saw immediately
in the shadow thrown ahead of me   by the sinking sun
that I was being followed   by a huge box.
Eliot said   it's possible to waste your time   and mess up
your life   for nothing.   I wish   He hadn't said that.
I wish   I had not taken it metaphorically   when She
traced a right angle in the air   out   over the pancakes
towards the roofs of 9th St.   saying of the old frame
          "The window   is falling
              out the window."

The little dwarf boy
is sitting in front
of the fire
eating an apple.

The peelings
perfectly cut
are wondrously winding
out of his left ear
as he eats.

FROGS RINGING GONGS IN A SKULL

(a netsuke)

Just as the term "beautiful woman"   is used
by those   who bored by the very image   don't
want to go into detail   Garbo's stunning forehead
has peeled   clear to the tip   of her nose
beside the elevated sign   "HOTEL"   where a silvered
snow is falling sideways   dark horizontal bars
between the stuttering flakes   Down here
we appear   Bound   in Dashes   Like
the guy   who after the 6th time   was easily caught by
the police   & questioned   Why he always robbed
the *same* donut shop   "I don't have a car," he told them
"& it's close to where I live   it's handy."
Easy to make the first mistake   & after that the rest
are simple   Or is it just the middle   of the story?
Where we look up   & see Laura Combes   who at the Best Woman
Bodybuilder competition   broke the ultimate taboo for
woman bodybuilders   by making a fist   when she flexed
her biceps   Like wood inlaid   with brass and antler
She   will never weep over the floral patterns on the
linoleum!   She will never trash the kitchen   She
will never be a griper   whining how she shoulda been
a dancer   she so tall   & all her bones are metacarpals!
She will never dress in yellow   & blendingly rose   Looking
like an after dinner mint!
                O Stupid
                   Stupid Beauty!
                The present has no history
                   but mine!

FROM *Zombie Notes* (1985)

> Under wrong trees
> walked the zombies
>
> — Stevie Smith

SARAN WRAP

        the other night at dinner   when you said
        "I've never known a famous writer   & I probably
        never will"   I experienced   "Future Shrink"   a
        wool sweater trounced in hot suds   or cotton too
        long under water   like Thomas Hardy   who found out
        he had fallen in love with   his own niece   not knowing
        she was the illegitimate child of the illegitimate daughter
        of his own mother   or saran wrap   in steam

"stone letter in a pot"

> Air picks a trail along these sills   where
> Instead of Adam & Eve   Fanny has typed Adam   & Even
> Though the rest of them will want you to go on "being
> a woman"
>
>
> I don't want to hear anything more about love   or
> See the word for centuries in every poem I read now
> Two cats sit in a circle of light   O baby
> I don't understand even in heroic summer
>
> Two frogs bleep from two separate ponds
> Soothing damp enters between fat bugs on my screen
> the hour is pie-eyed   Shutup   & hear the frogs

"stone letter in a pot" is a Japanese expression. When you're unable to say exactly what you mean, you say something else instead, and these substituted words are called "stone letters in a pot."

DAYS & NIGHTS

This is certainly not a painting   by Ni Tsan
a fourteenth century master   whose obsession was
cleanliness   his sparse landscapes   practically all
brush   & hardly any inkwash   But more
in the style of Shen Shih-ch'ung   his milky monochrome
The Pavilion of the Luxuriant Trees   where
two figures   discussing on a balcony   seem to be immersed
in a pile of Necco wafers
                     & you & I   go out of the house
& scream   "Fuck you!"   at each other   in an open field
hurling a bottle of Rolling Rock   (two good sips still left!)
into the dark   all because of a paragraph   in the
New York Times magazine section   describing   a
serious young woman machinist   as   "loving the arc
of the welding torch   and the flow of the molten
steel"   & I said   "sexist"   over your shoulder   & we
left the lake early.
                    Water
and a preparation of pine soot   & the pines   so thinly
arranged   the painter gazes   out of a wicker window
into rectangular fog   Obviously no one has ever
told him   he lacks depth perception!   Below
his spongy jowls   his palms   must be sleeping
on his knees   crushed   in the folds   of blue bamboo leaves.

Often the simplest words!   only take you to the edge
of the sea   where to the artist   you are merely a tall dot
who has run out of land

               or as Frank O'Hara once said to me
as we were strolling in   the tide
                 "Baby, this is weather! . . . . . .

for Bill Kushner

When he said   "petit air"   I thought the translation
would be   "little fart"   Some mornings it is cleansing
to lean from bed   lift the window   and scream   I HATE CHILDREN
into the lovely green yard.   It makes it possible   to
go downstairs   & answer Kyran's   "Mom!   mom   mom moms!" Lovingly
one thousand   one million   one hundred & forty four times   & Not
think the orange juice   suffers   in its fall   Just another
winter scene   in August   Like Ed's card   where   rouge   has been added
to the sky's cheeks   & the snowball queen   is wearing turquoise "pumps"
& embracing a bundle of cotton   shaped like snowballs   because it
is easy to write   easy poems   but more difficult   to write   more
difficult poems   which is not quite the same as saying   I'm not
interested in sex   unless I'm doing it   & not the same as
Kyran saying   "I like TV dinners   better'n I like TV"   But
somewhere in between the two   & why   this poem is titled

GRACE NOTE STUDY

On such a morning   you can wade through the bodies   of tiny khaki
army men   carrying   massive artillery   place your coffee beside
your typewriter   & begin a poem   No one
will leave you alone   because you are a mother   & When
you open the book on Calamity Jane   the first sentence   of the preface
will say   "No career is so elusive to the historian   as that of a
loose woman."

                    Reminds me of a story   on the radio
in Minnesota this summer
                    the song   it seems   was actually written about   a
                    boy   young heir to a supermarket chain   But they
                    made it a much more marketable item   by changing

the gender   Causing it to be about a   spoiled
& willful debutante

    this is a true story
    this is how they got a hit   45

"Can I Still Love You   & Hate the Word Husband"

   is it any wonder   when you've taken caffeine   sugar
red meat   & butter   out of your diet   you feel
something is missing . . . . or your dentist   checking
out your x-rays asks   "Is there anything that's bothering
you?"   & a terrible   silence falls . . . .   On Tuesday
a little fit arrived on a postcard saying   "Science
has ruined   all my sunsets"   as when he   hired a skywriter
to draw a   giant stem   & leaves around the sun   making it
the largest sunflower of all time!   it lasted less
than a minute   but So many people   are happy   in love
with lovers   sassy with idiosyncrasies of their children
relentless! to their daily tasks   & those
irritating harmonies!
       as in absent-minded   Kyran dropped
the washcloth into the toilet   just as he flushed. blueterry
in a whirling   but according to her   color scheme
my name is brown, red, gray, orange-red   green, green, gray
White, light brown, green   & gray   & I wish to mention
the trees   in this blue terry air   it's autumn   I
should have invited everyone   to give a Chinese honor
to a season   autumn viewing on the veranda   if we
had a veranda   but tea is possible   in the deepest blue
teapot   whose embossed bulges   tell us the myths & their
names   one more time
       Instead I woke into   the melancholy
of departure   where the wrong clock sentinels from a
balcony   or raised floor   supported by a series of pillars
some slit-wide flags blow sideways   but the train's steam
stops   in the immense pigment   & the road
could be   completely out of whack   it seems of wrong
perspective   & mistaken for a tower   with a train at the top
suggested flight   proves nothing   the train's not passing
through   & two   figures are flanked by insect shadows   they
got so small   from standing on the road to look even more so
out   of proportion   we know they have strolled   ¾'s of it

but   not to catch the train   they don't know they are so small
to know what they're doing   At least they have time to yawn
& be part   of the painter's enigma!   & I am merely crushed! by
Fall's dark beauty   whose trees are full of pterodactyls!

"It's impossible to get out of Ireland"   was what he said   to
me driving home last night.

Novembers   or straight life

    It's guys   like Emerson   that always fuck it up
    Who from his journals —marked for later use in
    Social Aims   under "Manners"   wrote

      My prayer to women would be, when the bell rings,
      when visitors arrive, sit like statues.

Impossible!   to give passionate head   after reading that!
Impossible   to blow you   under propelling tables!   our
beers whitecapping   on the nap   Oblivious!   of swizzle
sticks   & Cinzano ashtrays embedding   in our backs!
While the Pope hits a new low   & the Professor   who is so
brief   as to be left with nothing more to say   has rectified
this once again   by repeating everything three times . . . . . . even
a tree surgeon will bend over the fence   asking   "Is your
husband home?   Is your husband home?   Is your husband
home?"   as though you didn't hear him   instead of simply
choosing not to answer.   How To Talk To Assholes   was a
possible title I was considering   in honor of the doctor
studied my severely swollen thumb   & inquired   as to whether
any strenuous exercise had   been taken of late   "perhaps yanking
a fitted bedsheet over a mattress?"   he postulated . . . .
        "Is this a town?" I asked
        "Yes," said Uncle Alfred, "this is Raven Brook,
        and here is Jake waiting for us."

WE CAN'T FIND THE TRAITOR BUT OF COURSE
HE'S STAYING RIGHT HERE IN LONDON
AT THE WINDSOR HOTEL

        Calmly & with an air of detachment   she folded the great
ship in two   & sank it   . . . no
I must have imagined that   I must have imagined
the french fries   the wind aching over the hot rods
night's crushed geography   where all the wrong people
went off with the wrong people   I must have imagined the
air off the steeple's   dark point   where in telling her story
she seemed not to notice   that one by one all the men who
left her   became novelists   I must have imagined   someone
sent me her ring   in a small box   they said this is her ring
we thought you'd want to have it   but it wasn't her ring
I was dreaming again   I must have imagined the
motif of confronting birds   or pigs
who like sharks & children will put anything
into their mouths   the world considered in terms of
chewable & non-chewable   & then two days later the
cartoonist's spouse   committed suicide.   I must have imagined
the paper flew up from your hands!   the milk exploded
on the stove!   I must have imagined love was out of fashion
the spectators came to be shocked!   the knobs resembled
elephant's eyes   you always loved this weather.   Unlike
the horse   who relies on the assumption   that no one is
there   as to the sound of hay drifting on a thought
of hay   dreamed up & sent ceiling   I must have imagined
that we would go on calling it what it was meant to be when
we said it   & I would never need to measure the chairs to
make my point!   I who pounded on your dreams   &
walked backwards in snow to confuse you   I must have
imagined you were calling just to rub it in!

in my dream   my grandmother
maggie sullivan   has me by
both shirt sleeves   & is
agitating me up & down   "Use
Gerunds!"   she is screaming

Tutankhamun's coffin weighed 2,448 pounds and 2 ounces
Searching the original letters behind museum glass   I
noticed that Van Gogh had neglected   to cross
his t's
Do you remember saying   you dreamed you had shoes
inside your shoes?   I don't know why you stay by me
My straw   my sunny blond on blue   now pink   to
the color of almond flowers   as the baby climbs out
of bed   announcing   "I got dreams   all over me
got to   wash them off!"   Matter-of-factly he goes
throws water at his neck and arms . . . . misses . . . .
Outside   frizzled silhouettes poke the light   So
green   with a grey mist rising   in pointless
cloud disguise.   I plan not to move   the baby
thinks I'm still asleep   through slits I track
the know-it-all birds   actually they seem to.   As
for the rest of the philosophers   " . . . . nothing,"
Flannery O'Connor once wrote,   "produces silence
like experience . . . ."

A PIECE

        Well . . . .   I suppose I was talking   about how
he said to me "They called Jack Kerouac a sexist!"
So I said   I said   the thing is   I said   you
have to decide whether   you're going to overlook any
sexism   because you think he's such a great writer
So you put   the question   the whole question of sexism
aside when   you read him   and concentrate on the value
of the writing itself . . . . . I mean it doesn't alter the
fact   of his being sexist   that he was holocaustically
sexist. He wouldn't deny it I'm sure I said.   In
VISIONS OF CODY he talks about how   the woman takes
the "melted marble of man's sperm"   and transforms it
into   "a large bulky piece of   decayable meat" and
that as far as young women were concerned   he couldn't
look at them unless he tore off their clothes one by
one   and that   that was about all   all he could say
about all girls . . . . "and only further refinement is their
cunts and will do" he said.   Well . . . .
But then this guy said   to me   he said   "Yeah,
but you don't think he's sexist   do you?"

Because   Therefore   So

  If You Wear A Hat In The House
  You Are Warmer Than If You Don't

Because   it must be the baby speaking   petitioning
Jack's Mom   "But Mom . . . these beans are good beans
They're magic! . . . the old woman gave me . . . magic beans!"   It
is radiant   on his head   Apparently the heat in
the body slips through the holes in the skull   & Rises
that's why Sean O'Casey is always photographed   with
a hat on   But O Science   You ventriloquist!   Paroxysms
of sunlight   ignite   this blond mist of curls   & I
have to weep   for the sentimental   and maudlin   one last time!
tho the Southern New England Telephone Company   has delivered
a message   "That lucky ol' sun   just rolls around heaven all
day   but now it will be followed   every second
by a big silver saucer!"   Therefore by reflection
each shape completes itself   continues   along the
Silver Ridge Trail   traceable through the woods   by
the circular lids of tin cans   nailed to the trunks of the
Hemlocks   & Tulip.   So   I want to thank   the sheep
who has eaten all the maroon   & adjectival   the white
pine for not being white.   Now that I am master of the
dotted quarter note   preceding the eighth note   I thank
the baby   for pouring   into the small popsicle mold   the
large pitcher of grape juice   & Patrick   dressing
singing
            "I know a woman   named Lucky Pierre   she
            used to   cut   my hair.

Winter is so   punk.   It's Steel shades shaded tin   &these
strung-out Ash trees   their anorexic limbs   dovetailing
with the light.   I often go walking   with a second figure
we laugh   about how we both   should have taken up
painting instead.   Once
from an opposite crosswalk   We saluted   a man with
Fuchsia   for hair   A thatch the hue of Modern Magazine Pussy!
We chortled.   Winter is so punk
the sunlight's raw   & all the bushes   Seem to be
in poor health   sometimes you wish
you still knew the people you used to know
better

                    I was still stirring the noodles
when he threw the broccoli back into the frying pan
& the fight was on!   It must be a sign
that the disappointments of life   are setting in.
We lolled in the hay til noon   intellectually discussing
passion   You can't blame short hair for everything!
Remember when the word   moonlight meant romance   &
now   it just means   holding down two jobs
                                            My
uncle Trap   got layed-off the track   for five years for
doping horses   As a kid I used to hold   them for him
Shank in hand   I'd ask   "How come you give them a shot   before
they run?"
              to make a constellation   he'd say   into which
or upon   which   other constellations fit   or are placed
unfitted   & are cut   by circumstance to fit
                        other times he'd just say
                                            "Vitamins."

Poems Without Names   or your plane takes off

The difficulty lies   in telling   which card
is the ace-in-the-hole   he said he knew a woman who
wired her mouth shut   to lose weight   Dear S What I
thought was   maybe I could go to China   where on the front
of this card   the women seem to work hand   in hand   with the
men   Nevertheless we can't see what we look like from behind
& tomorrow is full of people who   think I'm weird   & a creep   &
They are all   the Cousins   On a narrow street
firefighters   arch swoons   of water   into the feverish
amphitheatre   An analogy is made between fire & flowers
because tomorrow is full of people who   think I'm a creep
& they are all tear-shaped   because tomorrow is full of
personae who   think of me as analogy   trapeze domestic
or
      the little grocery hummed
      cops wilted blue

because tomorrow is full of people who don't want to mention
the enormous can of garbage   glued to their chests   "This"
is the reason   E pointed out   the angelic shore of the past
"Pigs ran on the beaches   you couldn't take off your clothes   or
they'd eat them"

& why the reader's digest   is like the Pope

            for Ulysses on his high school
            graduation

Just come home when you need to   or how does light get
between the stars   if there's no electro magnetic forces
in space

A small roaring in the foliage   of poplar &
reed   heat throbbing upward over the damp gravel
the last clump of tulips falls apart   Grey Tropical . .
. . . Yes   it's true!   Basically   you have
to learn what life is about   from the vertebrae pattern
of a frog!   all that remains is to be mentioned   or
don't put cast iron   in a sink full of suds overnight   &
if you can't speak to them in real language   always
use code.   Suppose this mist centered on stage left &
demanded our attention   because when everything was finally
settled   one of the dates got switched   & it all had to be
rearranged again   But O you are so beautiful   staring
out the train window   Saying
            "I hate Liza Minnelli!"

from LETTERS TO THE LETTERS S AND F
for Suki & Fanny

Tuesday   the first letter

Dear S

Today I didn't agree with what I said yesterday   to you
about having children   or not having children   Except
that I love these three   Even as   she will always sing
the praises of every tiny horrible aspect of being a mother   that I
hate   Sometimes I think I've learned   everything I know
Kyran explained at breakfast   how if you have a diaper on   you
don't need to wear underwear   & WCBS New York told about a man
completely on fire   who was rescued by his wife   She

put out the flames   with a garden hose   Now & then   a spouse
comes in handy   The air is full of light   & today I
received mail from   The Blinded Veterans Association, The American Lung
Association, Connecticut Light & Power, Bob Holman, DISCOVER (the news
magazine of science) sub titled   "Can A Heart Attack Be Stopped," Katharine
Hepburn, The Abortion Fund, Wausau Underwriters Insurance Company, Ronald
Reagan, National Women's Health Network, The Print Center, Manuscripts from
Albany, Lynn, MA, Columbia, & Atlanta,   a card from Helen Adam just back
from Germany en route to Arizona   & another graced package from Tom
Weigel   w/a note   Bob's card is a Winter Sunrise in the Grand Tetons   tho
it is August here . . . .

She taught herself   how to draw   in this garden   that summer.

Wednesday   October 14

Dear F

Crashed into bed 2:30a.m.   Crushed the alarm at 6:15.   Had
been dreaming of poetry   the different approaches   the last
line remembered in my head   "I belong to the blood"   Does this
mean I'll never be a   "language" poet?   Trying to recall more
of the dream   but T   suddenly announced he'd changed his schedule
this week & we had to get up!   Kyran to be picked up at 7.   Cold
& exhaustion are a miserable combination.   Pitch outside.   Some
get up at 4a.m. every day of their lives.   Nuns & Priests never
sleep late.   Buddhist monks have swept six temples before dawn.   Some
times the beauty of the empty avenue . . . . but so cruel!   to the body
the pitiful   frame shoved upright into stinging air   shaking & stumbling
the little hoarse voice wailing over the simplest of structures . . . .
"can't find my socks . . . "   The house a sea of moans and groans   The dead
getting out of their casks   painfully unbending   on the day of final
judgement   Then a
Radio   a ray of light across millions of miles sways down
between branches   & ignites   pancakes

Today I mail books, DRASTIC MEASURES, SUMMER SLEEPER
MYTHOLOGIZING ALWAYS, and some more AUDREYs.

I pull the jeep up behind the post office and lick stamps   I
stack long towers of manila envelops on the pull cart to take
inside. The light is brilliant   the leaves hop   off the trees.
Across the street they are looping and careening down   a young
guy is high up on a ladder-like scaffolding   his partner is
below   hoisting boards up   the house is getting a new side   it
is so clean   so clean   the air so clean   & sharp   Corners
of light   make my eyes smart   the leaves are gorgeous   the house
is huge old wooden & gorgeous the scaffolding   the truck parked
shiny and black   & battered just so   the disorder of the tools in
their neat stacks   each one so gorgeous   the brown hair of   the shining
young carpenter he is so gorgeous   his partner's hands on the boards

are   singing   it is all so gorgeous the leaves have set out on a
journey   Under its great yellow load   the road   grey &
rises in a wing   towards the sea & in the horrible deep of   my heart
I know I want it back   the having no place to live   no home   the
homelessness   the terrible cruel happiness Patrick saying   "I
always think of that summer   that song   we didn't know who we were
we   didn't know   where we were going . . . . we were just
on the road . . . . "

Wednesday   November 11

Dear F

Tonight missing John Cage at the Poetry Project.   There is something
very John Cage   about missing John Cage   but I regret I am not there
to see his wisdom   and hear him chuckle at himself for appearing as
himself.

Just now you called sounding depressed. I'm no puff ball myself these
days what with looking for a job and all. I want to feel   like
Patrick   who just came through the room saying he   should study for
his Spanish final, but he'd end up watching the hockey game instead.
"I have no control over what I do," he tells me.   "I like taking
life as a big joke   because it is."   Myself I   have always been
too serious   I boycotted the royal wedding   Refusing to even
watch the interviews with Prince C and Lady D on the telly   For
Lynch & Doherty! in British prison   for
Bernadette McDonnell   beside her starved father
's coffin   For the desperate rioting poor   in the streets of
London!   I boycotted the royal wedding!   I wanted to call
attention   to my cause by flying the Irish flag from the roof, but I
couldn't get hold of a flag   I thought of posting an announcement
"WEDDING BOYCOTT HERE!"   but who would see it jetting by in their
Subarus & pickups   So my boycott went on without notice . . . . .
. . . . Except for those unlucky few   who
had to listen to me berate them for their obvious bedazzlement with
royalty as they sat all ears to hear prince C   nasal
his secret   on how he has managed to just not go "mad"   living
with the eyes of the world on his every move!

                                                    Life's Tough
all over Baby I thought   some people can't even get noticed dying
of hunger   in an English prison
But it was over with a bang   wasn't it   & now Thanksgiving
is for certain   We will bring all delicious side effects   & wear our
Halloween costumes   I am a huge parrot w/wild red-orange   & yellow head
in my long black w/red velvet inside cape   or as someone suggested
as we were T or t ing   a volcano . . . .

Monday   November 23

    Dear F

                                             The yellow pigments
of the marsh   were becoming blue with the tide   the air was like
the corners of a large transparent box   those leggy reeds
she told me were called Johnson Grass in the south   Blazed
palomino   but despite the fierceness of the caption   "Cold"
under the picture   I am still unable to find a place for
Vladimir's line: "His eyes burned like a pair of angry assholes
in the snow."   If Arthur Conan Doyle had written like that   do
you think Sherlock Holmes would have been changed appreciably?
Patrick & I have just finished The Speckled Band   a grizzly
tale of murder   & are now reading one that involves a young
hydraulic engineer   whose thumb has been completely hacked away
not much different than the morning news on WCBS   Except
that Holmes is often emotional & acts like he 's just snorted
enough coke for 4 normal people   Then coming by Cox
School   I saw   the gangster woman   with her face from the
Dick Tracy comic strip   the same 3 deep lateral grooves on
each side   &the same   yellow hair   intense
as today's light
                      Cadmium

FROM *Imaginary Income* (1992)

"Women do two-thirds of the world's work, get one-tenth of its income, and own less than one-hundredth of its property."
— United Nations report

Place both palms on the floor & rotate
your body until you have become a large
feathered fan   explain
to the poll taker what   you think about
midnight vapors   bills and weather

sexuality because of sexism is a problem for most women

        if there could be a dinner
        perched on a hilltop in golden ash
        sullen   harmless   & forever uneaten

        the one who has gone ahead
        could be a scene behind glass
        in the museum of the future

        Otherwise
        a group of men paint themselves
        wild purslane
        yellow flower
        with succulent leaves

        & the woman in the green & white checkered
        housedress   stands in the doorway of the cottage
        on the island in the metallic gun-powdered
        salt of the sea   & hollers   "Honey . . . . ."

Soffits & Fascias

    wild & keen over our cold gossip
    why do only the saddest people want to write
    O Rilke   log of my heart!

    bushy aster   crooked-stem aster   daisy fleabane
    wind knocked the locust tree over   panes rushed out
    of the window   the brakes went out on the car
    the dryer broke   the electricity swooned into my
    arms   "I got up & got kids to school all my life"
    said Alice Schroeder   mother of murderer
    Blond Cole Hunter   who shot Jane Campbell

    a woman on the edge of her seat   woman on the tip
    of the iceberg woman through the eye of a needle   Women
    were painting waves on the floor of the basketball
    court   they
    dealt not with domesticity but
    with war, politics, coffeehouse
    intrigues, exploration,   & murder   Consider
    the margin   the lake before the storm
    grand recipient of the shakes   I
    the quaking one   going from door to door
    in the halls of my own house

Blue Nile

Her excessive urge to plan every second of the
other person's day.
I guess he was inspired by her to do it.
She arrived at the hotel room finding him in a white towel &
dripping water — as they talked he returned to the bathroom &
proceeded to finish drying & begin dressing. As they chatted he
pulled on clothes until he'd completed his attire & promptly
swung open the door to the hall   Downstairs they chatted even
faster as he strode briskly through the lobby   & once outside
he told her he was glad she'd come by then he turned & bounded
off in another direction.
Freud told her her dreams were what he would
expect of a woman poet.
Becoming Famous & Powerful
Careless of all advice, flowers
she   remodeled her basement & did tricks she'd learned in
the circus referring to her life as the "Big Top"
In the tablets we turn to
"In white she was bathed"
Betrayed by the hand that held the mirror
Medusa's hair was snakes.   Was thought
split inward.

O
Orange & gum
visions of light over horses' backs   the backs of horses
I fly into your branches!   I erase my heart!
I carry the rafters on my skull
the remains of the house
windows drop from my shoulders   screens
& curtains crumble
white walls like plain flats   like a
soft run of marsh burst from bone structure!

something is always so beautiful
a man was running alongside the highway his
light shirt flapping   his slow brown stride
finally   it's the statement of lingering   the
hesitation in the rickrack of some lacy pattern
washed ashore — i.e.
I think I love him but maybe I just want to slug him in the nose!
I missed the talks   the speeches   the terrible
arguments   & worries

Spaces were in the great bodies of the trees   three
hats came by carrying flowers   breathless white lilies & a
bouquet like a design off a curtain in a 50s cafe in Sebastopol
my father was there   the worst of us   & yet
I remember him best

tall white & densely fluid

one night.   Starry.   a young woman trampled
clothes   in a stream   no ordinary laundress
she or I   to be bending
at the waist   as night is elegantly bent.

the night as night   elegant & starry
slightly bent at the waist   referential
several churches surround the green   tall white
boxes   sharp & quivering

Several churches surround the green.   Beside
the mailbox a miniature angel addressed my thumb.
trees jerked from the mist   hunks of dark smoke
It is possible to build a house without a door?

tall white boxes w/deep oblongs at center   face's
center   trace of infinity
of stars scraped the paint off the night as
night   a young woman trampling clothes in
a stream

tall white and densely fluid   deep at their
center   center of face   face's center rasp
in the navied air   trace
of infinity of stars   scraped the paint off
glued the doors shut   the box closed   the night as
night   a young woman trampling clothes in a stream.

Martha

        She threw her entire arm over her hat   while
        the butterflies were flung   past her
        eyes closed   lips pulled in.   She caught herself
        against the gust   swallows flipped   every which way
        white suddenly   as her dress and hat
        and the arm she locked straight out   she was
        holding on   to   some idea

seeing him's like standing on a hot plate
the immaculate returning

        It's not like you'd imagine midnight   sound
        of a car going past   whoosh   not like you're decked
        out & following   but more like   he only had
        one gown   and he wore it   everywhere

        Just a speck in a mote's eye   it would seem fit
        to be indifferent   What'll it be? she asked the stars
        plausibly disconnecting all memories of how blue the water
        felt when you leaned forward from rowing   or stood
        up in the boat shaking your empty wallet at the moon
        or for the moon to see   that's what they said
        shake your empty
        wallet for the moon and money will come your way

how I feel is cool   very cool

                      cold fills the south window
                      ice wells in the south window
                      snow drifts in the south window
                      icicles drape in the south window
                      a bitter wind
                      a frozen surge at the south window
                      the bitter   neck of winter is in the south window
                      the bitter neck of winter is in the south window

                      You hear the train go West in the south window
                      & then retire to bedlam   a wind would
                      come up a wind   stone of heart
                      would flower in icy petals over the window
                      in the south   over the south window

So muchos the story & tale it goes into oblivion
like raccoons   in the arms of children   bandit faces
& that little nose always looking for its share
so unpredictable   one day he'd be so friendly you'd
think for sure he had something in mind   then the
next time it would be all off   whatever it was . . .
as though he'd almost . . & then decided against it
So he controlled all your responses   by throwing his
voice in these manners   calling you here then sending
you there   all the while setting you up to invent his
emotions for him   to construct a route of passion he
could claim   as you like a crazy person darted back &
forth in the role of: both actors, the set & scenery,
the wind machine, an occasional song routine,   & a
personal narrator   who explained the feelings of both
characters being portrayed   as well as   their dogs!

Always the word "love" written in vanishing ink . . . vanishing
or
Edith wharton   is missing
for E. B.

      Turning the page   we witness how another survives.
      She takes the circular staircase   to the weathervane
      & that   puts her right on top   of the view
      the nightly ritual of standing in the front doorway
      breath pumping into the flat dark   We are staring
      at a sky the   color of a Parrot tulip   staring back
      eyeball to eyeball jagged star to jagged star   perfect
      bead to perfect bead   maybe low clean fog   or
      wet-washed air Orion   Big Dipper   venus mars?
      The door a thick slab of hard wood   chipped   painted &
      repainted   strata of each layer marking   an idea in
      progress.

      "I really am fine"   she wrote   "I went to Africa last
      June to see the Mountain Gorilla of Dwonda   I am very
      happy"   it's love at the base of it all   love stops
      the heart goes on   but love stops   Stops   Stop
      it!   love!   Stop it!

Dashboard Idol

or

Imbecility differs from idiocy. In idiocy the mind
is not developed; in imbecility it is imperfectly
developed. Idiocy is absence of mental power;
imbecility is feebleness of mental action. See Idiot
             story of

   Remember that night when the lights got up & walked
   on the water ice
   glazed on the streets seems cellophane What's
   real is not objects but the space around them your
   fevered body under the cool walnut trees Observe
   how multiplication is making dark circles in the atmosphere
   overhead blue water on the radio Stage
   for the illumination of a mirage inside the beat of
   the songs he really broke her heart dee dee dee dee da da
   she's waiting for a change of his dee dee dee dee
    well . . wasn't everyone like that? Wasn't a part
    of love the love of being in love in the first
    place?
Driving
  ice on the streets like
    porcelain pillows
Who showed up & why or the question is did he hate her
what did it mean that he avoided her what did it mean
that he said I hate you what did it mean was
something wrong with her or was the pop-up lizard real?
he couldn't arrive at the same party couldn't
make small talk couldn't be dark & rained on wet damp
was he bitter or merely cultivating abstraction?
Allow!
me to dream the dream of closing my eyes to subtract
a place & place it

We
watch the swimmers intermittently decapitated &
reinstated   decapitated & reinstated   whole
headless   whole headless

        love is not   one kind or another
        is fashioned of stumps   one so fleet of
        soup   one fictive as
        a cushion in a foolish melodrama
        one gaunt garish garrulous gander
        another seeks potato plots &
        several dig famously where the map
        has indicated fortune   one is a   giraffe
        space bursts open in a wound
        air cracks a corner hissing
        night reclines at the circus
        milk takes on the color of everyday
        stone rebukes the finder & shrivels up
        toast is like a taco for the rich
        beer makes you stupid
        beer makes us stupid   wine too
        see me about this later   Stupid
        water has a point
        water deserves better
        water is not burnt sienna or plain sienna or blue
        my cup   my shoes
        I fill my cup   I fill my shoes
        sand is not yellow or brown   or creme or white or
        black really
        sand is permanent   we sit on it
        from here   we see
            the bathers
            leave their feet at the edge of the lake

the happiest parts were the parts she made up

        Nothing there to pursue
        he's got a heart like an iron lung
        no sign of life   vapid fair & fairly

        "Meet us on the other side!" I shouted to
        the running boy   "Don't say that in here!"
        X blurted   as our little cart picked up speed
        on the cemetery path.

Talking to distract the listener.
or   Hanging out with the Beloved equals a festival

        I fold the blanket to end winter.   Cézanne said
        each part was as important as the whole   (so)   I
        bought a clock because it had Mexico (stamped) on
        the back
          I never dreamed I   held you in my arms.
        Certainly the sum of the parts is more   expensive   than
        the whole.   By mistake we invited a woman who'd just
        spent five years in a cloister   She was talking a
        mile a minute   Her mother
        saved clocks   clocks of all
        dimension   Who appointed herself Warden   of
        Punctuality   Collector of one
        through 12   Madonna of brass & porcelain inscribed in
        ordinary   & Roman numerals
        III   VII flipping forward   & Flung
        up behind   invention of wheel   of
        time   All circle of   "What goes around
        comes around nah nah"   mows down the home
        they made   mows down   mother's shelf
        charming end table of birds-eye maple   Walnut
        gnarled claws   swollen jadite   lucid
        obsidian basin   O Silent Faces O

        strange population!
                           Wound each would gain or lose
        & hourly sing   unsynchronized.   Then all the
        rooms would fill in clamoring festival of Bongs!
        so various   & drunken   with rhapsody in that music that

        has no notes

rain dents a steady robust
the great ghost flower sprawls
over the red lacquer poppy
tacked to the tar paper wall

rain dents a steady robust
the great ghost flower sprawls
over the red lacquer poppy
tacked to the tar paper wall

FROM *Untapped Maps* (1993)

"... but then I wouldn't long for anything
desire left in some abandoned suitcase
a train going West under the Big Dipper..."

to fly

            into a rage
            to be done with it
            to be lost in a holocaust
            of your own hideous design
            to arrive late & leave early
            to misunderstand the directions
            to fail to speak the same language as
            the eloquent orator
            to be at war at home & in the heart
            to disagree with everyone about the movie
            to be personally affronted by the drizzle
            to miss the last train
            to plan an elaborate excuse & not use it
            to receive a bouquet entirely of stems
            these   are some of my reasons

In August 1874 Manet stayed with Monet in Argenteuil
a village on the   Seine   only a brief train ride from Paris

        While Manet painted the Monet family
        Renoir painted beside him & Monet worked nearby
        Monet painted Renoir at his easel while
        Renoir like Manet painted Madame Monet

What do you do when you can't forget the one you
don't love anymore

       Somewhere in the night   water is bending its knees
       listen to the beeps & voices on the road or just
       stand at the little attic window late past midnight
       & not quite hear what the neighbors are saying as
       they come home noisy   & slam car doors

       it's not Cézanne shouting to his models   "Be an apple!
       Be an apple!"   when he arrived he came   from somewhere
       else   as a legend might   in a boxcar

Something just out of reach

that is   if he could loan her a saddle   he probably could loan her a horse

also ... tattered flag

> When Basho took a trip   he carried extra nightware
> lacquer filled the places that his foot went   O
> happy route   not torrid   or   ice encased
> not rushed nor motionless   or the office of oversight   &
> Investigations or of a spot beset   The just &   mismapped
> intersections of the trails   Now   you go your way   &
> I go mine   like a great waste of information!   While
> following a series of calamities   Calamity Jane
> arrives in the mail   from calamity you   to
> calamity me   the self returning in pieces
> like parts blown into outer space having made the big circle
> You said one thing   I thought
> you thought another   truer message   you couldn't say   So
> this metaphoric ruse   called home   That lacquer
> spilled on a distant planet   surfacing the outline
> we aspire to   our nature is forbidden compensation
> or forbearance of trust   reality's
> illusion blows the music to a high pitch   & we may
> then weep or tremble   or sit ajar   abandoned
> at the local station   trains   waving
> But Basho walked everywhere   skeleton
> holding the body together   the rest pure technique
> Perpendicular light   through bamboo trunks
> Mountain villages perched like chickens on a roost

Maybe the stars were crossed   the night   winded

or

generalized uncertainties

>   At the hem of twilight   she has flung the carrot tops
>   soft arms & elbows mustered   everything changing
>   Honey put your dark side on   & grease the road with muddied
>   orchard light   O lowly amber shell of duck
>   & let there be cattle of various colors as I was
>   always seeing in that time   a chewed grove of trees.
>   She thinks fools names appear in public places
>   she thinks you can't cut your losses
>   she's rather stoic   & big boned
>   she thinks they left her because she wanted to be alone
>   she thinks she has to keep moving because she isn't lost yet
>   she thinks stunning patterns divide
>   behind the eyes of the disinherited   she says
>   hey kids we might have water   victory at sea
>   great splashes   the crops are saved
>   maybe it was the slant of the sun on something   amber
>   over her shoulder someone is humming   someone is
>   asking what color her eyes are   dreams of accomplishment
>   where *are* all the French women poets!   Last night   she
>   introduced someone to their own lover   & now
>
>   this view

for Mary Kelly

FROM GOSSIP NOTES OF COURT LIFE   or THE IRISES OF LOYANG

    Originally   & through the thick of it   that was my plan
    & while there may be a beauty to just getting up & leaving
    or going under   he promised to love her if she wrote a novel
    O Ambivalent Onyx!   Reckless diamonds   obsessed opal
    or Unplumbed tourmaline   the introduction said
    her young son sat   between her legs   as though he were
    her penis   So in the original story
    of Cinderella and the Glass Slipper   the slipper is
    made of fur   but the translator mistook   the french
    & translated it   as being made of glass   then
    you suppose yourself outside this window   cutting flowers
    we put them in the iris vase on the table
    fill it with cold water
    beads form on the Nile green enamel
    We wonder why anyone would assume everyone wants a penis
    O Murky Garnets   seething amethyst!   Difficult quartz
    Relentless emeralds!
    She puts her lips toward her fingers
    sheets on the line lift   & flatten   & now the author
    has agreed   to define a woman's genitalia   as an "absence"
    or "missing part"!   O
    Self-effacing citrine!   desperate obsidian!
    O sacrificing moonstone   Screaming jade!

a great sweep of taffeta were the irises of loyang

TRASH STARS

      Mostly it's the saturation of the cobalt   in her footsteps
      as she mows
      like looking for Blake   albums & a sexy haircut
      all on the same afternoon
      She stares down into the green   dark & wonderful
      behind her the grass doesn't seem damaged   only shorter
      she thinks about space age whales scorched on museum walls
      in a nearby field bland barns   that float & whistle
      she thinks her best friends secretly detest the very
      heroheroines they think they're supposed to like   then
      for no reason   she remembers   Lydia   a
      postcard tucked into her bureau mirror frame   a
      photo of Mina Loy   taken by Man Ray
      he used   a thermometer

for Libby Riddles

Anchorage to Nome

What represents the reality   as the glove on the
train tracks a severed hand   is   that reality
to the observer   but the object lacks the history
of what it represents

Holed-up in Shaktoolik male mushers
said she was   "silly"   to forge on alone
in the blizzard

to the observer the symbol becomes what it touches off
but to the object itself
but it lacks the history of
but the symbol lacks the history of the original object

"I left those guys in my dust," she chortled
who looks at the symbol sees the same as what it stands
for
but this is superficial as the history is gone from the
new story
massive white before her
& chalk deadlines   When they closed their eyes
each dog thought of palm trees
don't let them forget!   don't forget!   let me know.

FOR KYRAN

      where we dream   & close our eyes there's
      no floor to speak of   see how we
      crawl across the rafters   balance on the
      beams   under us there is only the ceiling
      of the room below   over us   stars

      the boy caught the falling baby   he caught
      the baby in the air   the sidewalk imminent

      if they ask you how you   get to bed
      you just tell them you   step lightly

I had eaten too much sugar
I had eaten too much salt
I had said the wrong thing &
I had done the wrong thing &
I was shouting at the sea
folded and enfolded like a blue grain cut for harvest
because I wanted to walk   out onto it between the rows
& keep walking   until I arrived in Morocco

STANDING BEAUTY WITH SLEEVE IN   HER MOUTH   OR

a good title is usually brief

Dressed in ink   colour and gofun on paper   Salmon
&   tremulous White Peonies   continuous as the
snow   falling into the cat's warm milk   around
such silk of   tiny navy tinted donuts   printed in
proliferation   She's not a sister of Mercy

Dressed in   ink   colour and gofun on paper   salmon
clouds burst on her dark sleeves   and tremulous white Peonies
underneath a silk of tiny navy-tinted donuts printed   in
proliferation   She's like the snow   falling into the
cat's warm milk   or Kyran painting all his pictures
with white out   Blanc en blanc veneered of heavy snow   so
Lift & Swing   as the kimonoed arm inside its cloth   has
swayed upward

of ink colour and gofun   on paper   Salmon cloud bursts
on her grape sleeves   & tremulous white peonies   all
undersides white silk   & lastly the robe of tiny navy tinted
donuts
            STANDING BEAUTY WITH SLEEVE IN HER MOUTH
We imagine we think we know what someone is thinking we're

Dressed
  in
        ink colour and gofun   on paper   salmon cloud bursts
& tremulous white peonies   All
undersides white silk   w/tiniest   donuts   printed
her face a small herd of pale birds   o Standing beauty w/
sleeve in her mouth
        continuous as the snow falling   into the cat's
warm milk!   the kimonoed arm inside its cloth
has swayed upward   into her face   startling a small herd of
white   We imagine we think we know   what someone

༄ 147

is thinking   for example:
                       You addressed the window from the bed
                       in the middle   of your line   "it's
                       a shame we're not in love   this   room
                       would be so romantic"
Well La De Da!   She's no
Sister of Mercy   & personally I'd rather be   in 1920
arrested & charged with prostitution   in the snowed streets
because   I'd been seen smoking cigarettes

                              What kind of urgency is this
Love anyway?

                       Salmon bursts   on her great

Dark Sleeves   & Patrick has put on his coat   to eat
ice cream   so much more simple than fucking

                                        many young
women were arrested & charged with prostitution they had
been seen smoking cigarettes in the snowed streets
                                        At least
Painting endures   & says "unknown" for the artist   tho
even the date   is available   We're all like the snow
falling into the cat's warm milk   Or
Kyran painting all his pictures   with white out   Tremulous
white peonies   without a trace!

                              So this snow
falls into the cat'
s warm milk   & Patrick puts on his jacket to eat
ice cream
                 Is love   only an urgency?

Kyran paints all his pictures   with white out
the snow   will do this too   & in the end it's painting
that endures   not the painted   kakemono   ink colour & gofun
on paper
                       or silk
                 her face a small   herd of white birds

                                        It was the way
you said it   that ticked me off   as though   you'd
declared an emergency   & then mumbled "forget it"
it is what causes   this Salubrious woman   to want to chew on
her sleeve ... So   my borrowed underwear   & her kimonoed
hand.   We're not the Sisters of Mercy!   & you're not
the band

for Meenah Abdus-Salaam & her children, Zainab, Hussein, Amna, Askia, and Fatima
& for all mothers & children who are being allowed to sink like stones through this economy

TOPOGRAPHY

       A woman throws her children
       A woman throws her children from a high window
       A woman rushes forward   toward her children
       a woman is throwing her children   she throws them out
       through a window   a woman is rushing forward
       with her children in her arms   she is tossing
       them one by one   tossing them into the air an
       airiness that greets them but they   they
       begin to fall   falling they slip from her hands
       her body slams the windowframe

       a woman is screaming   her children are raining
       her children are raining   she has watered our dreams
       with children   her babies falling toppling over
       sliding down a long transparent rope   she reels in
       until her hands are full of rope   and rope is coiled
       where she stands   naked except for rope

       Perhaps she has taught them to fly   & so flung
       them from her   to set them free   to raise them
       from dreariness   to encounter them in another place
       she was aiming at a target placed high up
        the dream opens with the dreamer standing in
       the upper rooms   a point of fixation at the top

       a woman throws her children   she has pushed them back
       wards   or forwards   or
       lifted them bodily   & shoved   or grappled in
       hands arms & hair   and wrenched them from the floor
       & bumped   or held them tenderly for just

a second   in her arms   the sky is full of children
she teaches them travel   the one final move
the upward maneuver

a woman is throwing her children from
a fear of heights   climbing up a bank & becoming
paralyzed by fear to look back at the story below
she invents a perilous position   she is so heavy by then
she is in search of what is hiding   & wants to
know   closer to the ground the scene changes
becomes more subtle   more mysterious   & more defined

she was aiming at a target
it was placed high up
the dream opens with the dreamer
standing in an   upper room   the figure
at the top of the cliff is a symbol of the
outcome of 2 forces   & represents the most suitable
compromise   one thinks to condense its meaning
into symbols   but the resistance of the dream
seeks to satisfy its own demands
Descent

these children were coming down
vertical wheels of baptism   without the weight
lessness of astronauts without the tops of Acacia
trees woven into rainforests   without the imaginary
nets of molecules   with only the anchor of gravity

in one lump sum they divided it
they dreamed their mother catching them up
pulling them back through windows
into rooms furnished by their terror   walls
touched by birds   silken feathers of sounds
to fill their ears   like rushing traffic

in an amphitheater tiers   &
tiers of seats rise sleepily
to a considerable height
in a seat high up watching   a child has drawn

a house   the dream always opens with the dreamer
standing in the upper rooms   a point of fixation
at the top

often they stared at the blue ceiling
often the colors of the windows floating by
often their parched throats mistook the shimmering
of the glass for waters   tears flattened their cheeks
eyes blurred & wet   who wants to see the ants getting
larger   wearing pants & skirts   hats & shoes checkers
spill light over the ruins   the missing diamonds
perched like a soul under a floor lamp

a woman throws her children from a fifth floor
window   from a sixth floor   seventh   eighth floor
window   she says it's about angels   or about
the longing to be   a trapeze artist   the
circular dance
to say exactly where the fall   begins
where can it end then   exactly
the rain hammers down   but they walk

Verlaine   La Loca   Neruda   Tu Fu   Janine
Pommy Vega   Cesar Vallejo   Gertrude Stein
O lonesome Feldspear!   the outcome of 2 forces
Ride 2 horses at the same time
cross 2 rivers   drive 2 cars   Sing
2 songs Follow   2 dreams   A woman has thrown
her children away   she laid down in her life
& looked up   her arms ache   She cannot
account for misconduct   remorse   or   eventual
scandal   she canceled future

Buy 2 of everything in case
1 gets lost   ripped off or
damaged
Live in 2 houses   two apartments   Have
2 bathtubs
2 cats
2 ways of looking at things

see 2 counselors
Enjoy 2 lovers
visit 2 friends
understand twice as much
Know 2 routes to the destination
2 ways to put your foot down
2 ways to be standing
2 ways to pronounce "no"
2 ways to dress for walking
2 walks to take
2 kinds of exercise
Have 2 different saws   2 kegs of nails
2 hammers hanging   in 2 places
discuss 2 definitions of "Post Modern"
You can do twice as much
You can be in 2 places at the same time   A
woman   suddenly alone   in an empty room
walking   & falling   walking & falling   Now
with a floor   now without one.   Her scream
descending in her throats   all the way   to the street

Headlines read   "Mom suspends time"
no one knows what to do with it now   Now
that we know   a woman throws her children
Imaginer of what this momentum influences   this
strain of unraveling fragments   bent by calls
These children with the heavens for a parachute
Children of Alto-cumulus   Nimbo-stratus
Cirrus

this woman she left it for us   Her
coating of unresolved   her study of falling
the everlasting long depth   From the top you
are below   associated by miraculous timing
the shape of the yellow curtains blown inward
behind her eyes the pure geometry of horses graze
soft coats in winter static straight out   like
strings   holding them up in the world   level
in any direction

Because a child has drawn a house   with two windows
because the child has painted a house   a woman is
calling the names and the names of names   she is
calling through her teeth   her sleep   her dream to
undream the dream she is   The outline
of altitudes

Because a woman is throwing her children into outer
space   into other galaxies   anonymous solar systems
she removes them from chaos   into the lyric of motion
transfers them from seizures of terror to the oblivion
of spinning   something else   is on her mind

She thinks the air is liquid   she
dreams her children swimming   she dreams herself
dreaming   holding the hand of the swimmer
she dreams herself swimming with the dreamer
poised   at a great height
where the dream opens   the silence she is
after   the transmogrifying wind

What billows inflating sacks full of air
incomprehensible torrents of injustice flapping
which were you going   to remember at the moment
of your escape   she said she was   "Giving them
to God"   uncoined and shimmering   a river between
friends she was remarkable portraying the iconoclast
future of la iglesias white stucco   a cross of thick
pink and leaded blue   imitation emerald and jewels
banging the long sides   of telescopic nightmare

the table of that sleep   a cartoon likeness
posing star buckets   of hair of   burning glass.
Mom   of hair of logs and timbers   she's got hair
of burning glass
hysterical dogs and feathered beings swept about
silken air flowed internally where once a river
hesitated   stone space flung   this woman who is
falling backwards into time   who has forgotten
to dress

The unconscious motive   behind the dream
compares to the   conscious motive behind
an action   a means of escape

Waterfalls appear to her
a million tiny silver fish come flying
out of the jungle   aviaries full of pins
dropping   there is a contest of stillness then
in the trees   of who can move the least
Green fruit toppling   off a dish
port of force   or bias   Motive is
significant to the dreamer   representing a
tendency   constellations drip over the
low hem   of tunnels   stacked on end
slender escapements   spinning upward
small hands slipping from her shoulders
like a shawl

Neighbors say a Queen's woman's life was unraveling

because a mom threw her children   out of their
10th floor apartment   yesterday   in Far Rockaway

because in the photo   Police investigators are
shown taking measurements   of the window   because

firefighters had to guess which apartment the children
were falling from   because "she was the last one

you would expect this of"   because "she was mumbling
Mohammed Elijah & she   was going to jump also"

because a neighbor looked out in time to see the girl slide
& fall   "The mother pushed her"   he said

Woman with a vision   Who
can say enough to you now
the entrance to your grammers   scorched desert
Because you are mad   you can rejoice in it!
ear to the floor rattling   you hear

the circle scraping   the pounding door
a madwoman can't blame anyone   can't plan
an escape   because you are mad
fibers sigh for them   O Children
your mother is mad   is
this dark wind   this intrusion.

How do you feel   Mother
they've   plunged

the event occurs in the vision of itself
consequence waits in the wings   broader
wider than anything

Woman with a jungle in the shape   of a blouse
furious outposts   are the tale of the dream
wherein the tissue   of the dreamer is woven
as though the artist forgot to stop drawing
a woman is throwing her kids   she touches them
forces them out "Go, go, God's
waiting for you."

there is a window in the wall of a building
a building made of many floors   many floors up
room after room above   A woman is throwing
her children from   out of a high   window
Mother & children appear   lugging an anchor
no father in the cards
she takes   the neighbors by surprise

O kids
in positions of exile   the
nature of which is a mystery to you
the point of application   has shifted
inwards   the dream offers a kind of criticism
Our journey was strange   much
of the ground lay on the surface

the air is cool now   coming with the tourmaline
destiny of loops   the somersaulting vagrancy of

closing eyes   she handed that to them   the soft dark
to hide in   Can we say   she flew into a rage   or they
soared into the air   there is some relationship
between the kind of accident the rider experiences and
the accident that forms the nucleus of the dream
the horse appears black   because of so much pigment
Nothing reflects that saturation   no one   no one
children absorbed into a color   until she throws them
one by one   into the light

Designed by
Samuel Retsov

Text: 10pt Sabon

acid-free paper

Printed by
McNaughton & Gunn